THE GOLDEN SCEPTRE

Other Puritan Classics from Solid Ground

In addition to *The Golden Sceptre* you hold in your hand, Solid Ground is delighted to be able to offer the following Puritan Classics—

A BODY OF DIVINITY by James Ussher
**A COMPLETE BODY OF DIVINITY by Thomas Watson
Christian's Present for All Seasons: Thoughts of Eminent Divines
THE CHRISTIAN WARFARE by John Downame
**CLASSIC PURITAN NT COMMENTARY by John Trapp
**Commentary on Hebrews by William Gouge, 2 Volumes
**Commentary on Second Peter by Thomas Adams
Communicant's Companion, The by Matthew Henry
**Exposition of the Epistle of Jude by William Jenkyn
An Exposition of the Ten Commandments by Ezekiel Hopkins
FAREWELL SERMONS by Baxter, Brooks, Caryl, Manton, Watson etc.
Gospel Sonnets by Ralph Erskine
The Harmony of the Divine Attributes by William Bates
Heaven Upon Earth: Jesus, Best Friend in Worst Times, James Janeway
THE MARROW OF TRUE JUSTIFICATION by Benjamin Keach
Redeemer's Tears Wept Over the Lost, The by John Howe
Scriptural Exposition of the Baptist Catechism by Benjamin Beddome
Secret of Communion with God by Matthew Henry
A Short Explanation of Hebrews by David Dickson
The Travels of True Godliness by Benjamin Keach
** denotes a hardcover volume

THE GOLDEN SCEPTRE
HELD FORTH TO THE HUMBLE

A Classic Exposition of 2 Chronicles 7:14

JOHN PRESTON

SOLID GROUND CHRISTIAN BOOKS
BIRMINGHAM, ALABAMA USA

SOLID GROUND CHRISTIAN BOOKS
PO Box 660132
Vestavia Hills, AL 35266
(205) 443-0311
mike.sgcb@gmail.com
http://www.solid-ground-books.com

THE GOLDEN SCEPTRE: Held Out to the Humble
A Classic Exposition of 2nd Chronicles 7:14

by John Preston

FIRST SOLID GROUND EDITION – October 2016

Taken from the 1990 Edition by Soli Deo Gloria
Reprinted in London by The Religious Tract Society in 1837

Cover Design by Borgo Design, Tuscaloosa, Alabama

ISBN: 978-159925-364-0

Table of Contents

Introductory Exposition of 2 Chronicles 7:14		1
Section 1	On Affliction	2
Section 2	On Humiliation	58
Section 3	On Seeking God's Face	116
Section 4	On Turning from Evil	160
Section 5	Forgiveness to Those Who are Humble and Forsake Their Sin	215
Section 6	Sin the Cause of All Calamities	237

THE
GOLDEN SCEPTRE.

2 CHRON. VII. 14.

IF MY PEOPLE WHICH ARE CALLED BY MY NAME, SHALL HUMBLE THEMSELVES, AND PRAY, AND SEEK MY FACE, AND TURN FROM THEIR WICKED WAYS; THEN WILL I HEAR FROM HEAVEN, AND WILL FORGIVE THEIR SIN, AND WILL HEAL THEIR LAND.

These words contain the answer God gave to Solomon's prayer, which he made when he dedicated the temple. His prayer was, that when they prayed on earth, God would hear in heaven; and God promiseth, in the words I have read, to do all that Solomon asketh; which promise contains three parts: First, that He would hear in heaven; which phrase denotes either his power, that he is able to bring to pass what he assents to do. Men are said to hear on earth, because they can do little; but God in heaven. Or else it implies, that though he seems to be far off from his people, yea, though in heaven, yet he will hear at last. The second part is, that he will pardon their sins; and it is of all other mercies the greatest, for sin hinders all good things, and openeth a gap to all evils, and therefore David saith, " Blessed is the man whose transgression is forgiven." Of all requests it is the greatest that we can make, and of all grants the greatest that God vouchsafeth. Thirdly, he will heal their land, and remove their affliction: now observe the order of this, in that before he doth it, he pardons their sin.

Now this promise is further set forth by two things. First, the persons to whom it is made,—the people of Israel and Judah, notified by two attributes; 1 They are his people. 2. Called by his name, or on whom his name is called; as the name of the husband is called upon the wife, or of the father upon the sons; and as they in Antioch, and we, are called christians from Christ. Secondly, the conditions this promise is made upon, for it is the Lord's manner to put promises upon conditions. 1. If they be humbled, and humble themselves. 2. If that humiliation be not contained within the compass of their breasts only, but expressed by prayer and confession of sins. 3. If they "seek my face;" seek to be reconciled, seek his presence as separated from all things else, not seeking corn, wine, oil, but God himself. 4. If they part with their sins in seeking, for they cannot maintain communion with him else, for God dwells in light, and he who walks in darkness, can have no fellowship with him, 1 John i. 6, 7. And thus you have the analysis of the words: we in handling them will not use this method, but begin with the words as they lie.

Sec. I.—ON AFFLICTION.

We will observe first these three doctrines from these words, "If my people, called by my name:"

First, God sends sharp afflictions on his own people.

This appears by the coherence, for in the words before the text, "If I send plague," &c. then "If my people," &c.

Secondly, that yet in them the Lord is very tender and full of compassion to his people.

This loving compellation, "my people" argues as much; it is as if he should say, I cannot forget you, for you are called by my name; you are mine, though I thus punish you.

Thirdly, that the Lord's name is called upon his people.

For the first, the scripture is frequent in examples of this kind, so as I shall not need to stand to name any places to you, they are so well known already, I shall state some reasons for it, why it is so.

1. God sends sharp afflictions on his own people because he loves them, they are such as belong to him; and the ground of this reason is, because "anger is caused as much by love as hatred." It is a true rule, though it may seem a paradox, because when one loves another he desires much from the party beloved, and expects much from him, and therefore a cross and stubborn action from such a one provokes more to anger than from any other man; as from a son, from a friend, or from a wife, it woundeth more; and therefore God saith of himself, that he is "a jealous God." Jealousy is a mixed affection of love and anger: the meaning is, If I find my people's affection stealing out from me, I am presently affected, as a jealous husband useth to be in such a case; and there is no anger like unto that, nor none sooner stirred. God will endure ten times as much from another, but when one that he hath taken into covenant with him offends him, he is angry, and will therefore be sure to send some sharp

affliction on him, which is the fruit of his anger, for his anger is not in vain.

2. He doth it that his name might not be blasphemed. That was the reason he gives, why he punished David when he committed adultery; for the Lord must of necessity do it for their sakes that stand by and look on, to show to them that he cannot endure such things, no, not in his own people.

3. Because he hath said, that he "will be sanctified of all that come nigh to him;" he will have them know that he is a holy God, hating iniquity; and that none should draw nigh to him, but such as have holy hearts and pure hands. This was the reason why he sent fire upon Korah, Dathan, and Abiram; "The Lord hath separated you, to bring you near to himself," Num. xvi. 9, saith Moses to them, and that in the nearest manner, to do service as priests, to offer sacrifice, and you are among the heads of the people, and therefore he will not forbear you. Others that are afar off, it may be, God will long spare; but of those that are sanctified to the Lord, and draw near to him in profession and in the opinion of others, God will be sanctified by their bringing holy hearts before him, or else he will vindicate his holiness by punishing them, and will not suffer them to go on with profane hearts.

4. Because they are his people among whom he walks, and with whom he dwells; he is conversant among them: see 2 Cor. vi. 16—18, and the beginning of chap. vii. But you will say, Is he not everywhere else? Yes, but he is there as a man is in his own house, among his sons and daughters, observing every thing, looking narrowly to them; and because he is still with them, therefore he will endure no uncleanness among them. God will be sure to plough

his own ground, whatsoever becomes of the waste; to weed his own garden, though the rest of the world should be let alone to grow wild.

But you will object and say, That the saints often sin, and afflictions do not follow

I answer, It may be, and doth often fall out; and the reason is, because God finds his work done to his hand. If they plough themselves up, God will not; but if we do it by halves, (as that is our fault if we leave many balks behind us,) then God always comes with afflictions; yet then the less that you leave behind unploughed, the less will God afflict you. If you humble yourselves thoroughly, you shall escape, except only in the case of scandal, and then God must needs do it for their sakes that look on; as in David, God would have all the world see his punishment on him, as well as they knew of his sin. But this comfort you may have, though you have greatly sinned, if not scandalously, that if you humble yourselves thoroughly, you shall escape.

Use 1. Learn from hence to fear the Lord, to tremble at his words, and seeing he will endure no uncleanness in his own people, "stand in awe, and sin not." Labour to bring your hearts to such a constitution, to such an awful respect as to fear to omit any known duty, or to commit the least sin; and this had need to be urged upon you, for it is the cause of all laxness and looseness in our profession, that we do not fear the Lord as we should. If we had the "fear of God before our eyes," as the apostle speaks, Rom. iii. 18, that is, if we saw the Lord so as to fear him, we should walk warily, and look how and where we set every step; and the reason why you are so uneven and not like yourselves, is from want of the fear of the Lord. Now the reason of that phrase of the apostle, that the fear of God is said to be before your eyes, is from the nature of fear; as if a man be busy about anything, if there be anything that he fears, he will still have an eye to that, and he watcheth lest it should come with some bye blow, when he thinks not of it. And so doth the fear of the Lord work where it is, it fasteneth our eyes on him; and if the Lord were thus before our eyes to fear him, it would make us walk more evenly and more constantly with him. And therefore when the Holy Ghost in scripture would choose to commend a man, he singles out especially this property of fearing God; as that Job was an "upright man, fearing God." So speaking of Cornelius, it is said that he was " a just man, fearing God." So Abraham, when he would express the wickedness of the court of Abimelech, says, " The fear of the Lord is not in this place;" that is, there is no religion nor good men, God is not regarded there; and the more fear, the less sin; " Stand in awe, and sin not," Psa. iv. 4. If a man stand in awe of the Lord, he would be afraid of every sin; he would be afraid of vain thoughts, of being vain in his speeches, and of giving way to the least wickedness; afraid of every inordinate affection; he would be afraid how he spent the time from morning till night, and how to give an account thereof: afraid of recreations, lest he should sleep too much, or sleep too little, eat too much, or eat too little, as knowing all is but to whet the scythe to make him the fitter for his harvest work, and therefore would be afraid to forbear refreshments too much, or to use them too little. I beseech you, therefore, that are in covenant with the Lord, and nearest to him, that know yourselves to be within the covenant to consider this, and learn to fear.

And to help you in this, take two places of scripture, "If you call on the Father, who, without respect of persons, judgeth according to every man's work, pass the time of your sojourning here in fear," 1 Pet. i. 17; that is, seeing you have such a Father that judgeth every person, all his children, he will certainly afflict you if you offend him; therefore fear to do it. The other is, Heb. xii. 28, 29, "Let us serve God with reverence and godly fear: for our God is a consuming fire." "Our God," whom we worship, is not made all of mercy, he hath other attributes joined with it: to you he is a consuming fire, if you will not serve him with fear, though not immediately to consume you utterly, yet to afflict you, and thereby to consume your lusts; so that it is a dangerous thing to be negligent of him, to meddle with Him who is a consuming fire.

How sharply did God deal with David, who was yet nearer to him than any of us! First he took away the child from him, which to him was a sharp affliction, he being a tender father, and had a strong affection to his life, as appears by his fastings; and the like he had to Absalom, who yet was a rebel against him; and then to have almost all the people to fall from him, when he was an old king, and the sword never to depart from his house: all these sat close to him, went near his soul; besides his shame, to have his sin discovered to all the world, as appears by Psa. li. Have not we cause then to spend our time in fear, if he dealt thus with David? And do not say, That though he dealt thus with David offending him, that yet he will not do thus with me; for is he not a Father that judgeth all his sons, and that, "without respect of persons," as the apostle saith? Consider also what he did to Jacob and Rebekah for consulting and agreeing to get the blessing by a lie; for though the thing she went about was good and they had a warrant for it, and their end was good, yet they used ill means—a lie. But God met with them both for it: Jacob was therefore put to live twenty years away from his mother's house; whereas he should have staid God's leisure, and not have been too hasty for the accomplishment of that promise, for "he that believeth doth not make haste." And so God promiseth riches and all good things to his children, as much as they need, but they must not make haste, that is their fault. And when Jacob was coming home again, what a fear was he put to from Esau! that lie of his being the cause of their falling out. And how did Rebekah also for all that while want the comfort of a son she loved, and had none to live with but Esau! And so Moses was dearer to God than any man upon earth; he never spake with any face to face as with him, yet he would have slain him at the inn, for not circumcising his child; and also because of that other sin at the waters of Meribah he chooseth an affliction for him, wherein he most of all crossed his desires, denying him to go into the land of Canaan. It may be some small affliction in show, as this seemed to be, which yet pincheth sorely, and some great affliction, on the contrary, in bulk to others, that is not so to him that bears it. And thus he also deals with Eli, a zealous man; for when news was brought that his sons were dead, and many of the people slain, he was not so much troubled at this, as that the ark of the Lord was taken, and this amazed him so as that he fell backward, and brake his neck. You see the holiness of the man; yet because he had preferred his sons before the Lord, and did not govern them well, God did not only thus take away his sons and his life, but the priesthood also from his house for ever: and have not we then all cause to fear? How did God deal with the good prophet that was slain by a lion? His fault was that he believed another man's word, pretending that he had God's word, when he had God's word expressly given to himself. This sin was as the sin of Eve, who believed the devil's word, when she had God's word expressly: therefore let us when we have the word of the Lord stick close to it. And so however he deal with Gideon, a worthy man, reckoned up among those worthies, Heb. xi. yet when he made an ephod, see what judgment fell upon his children, and all his house was cut off, Judges viii.

These examples are useful for you to consider, that you might know and fear the Lord; for the want of this is the cause of remissness and looseness in our profession, and that we do not so consider our ways. St. Paul was a holy man, and one that was on near terms with Jesus Christ, yet he feared exceedingly; "Knowing the terror of the Lord we persuade men," 2 Cor. v. 11. And Job, who was very exact in his life, as appears by chap. xxxi. (which chapter is nothing else but an expression of the manner of his carriage,) gives this as a reason, "For destruction from God was a terror to me;" and so in verse 2, the reason why he would not give liberty to his eyes to look on a maid, was that he considered, "What portion of God is there from above? and what inheritance of the Almighty from on high?" This fear of the Lord is needful at this time, when God hath discovered himself to be angry with the land; which is not only for the gross sins of wicked men, but the sins of the saints also; for their coldness, remissness, and laxness. I have two grounds for it: first in Rev. ii. because Ephesus was fallen from her first love, therefore he would remove her candlestick, that is, the whole church among them, and carry them into captivity; (for I cannot see by the candlestick how only the ministry should be meant.) So in Rev. iii. because Laodicea was neither hot nor cold, therefore will " I spue thee out of my mouth." God would endure them no longer; and therefore you that think your state the best, even you have had a hand in this plague; you think that other men's sins, the sins of wicked men, are the cause of it, but God knoweth, that they cannot pray and have no life in them, as you have; and though their sins also be a cause, and a main cause, as appears by the Amorites, whose sins, when full, God punished; yet I say they are yours also. And therefore, when there is an evident sign, that God hath a controversy with a kingdom and the churches, and a sign of his wrath is proclaimed from heaven, then every man must do something. Now fear the Lord, be zealous, repent and do your first works; begin now to mend your pace to heaven. And yet would there were only a want of zeal among you; yea, is it not in disgrace? is not a zealous man hooted at, as an owl among us? The excellency of it is exceedingly abated and eclipsed, the zeal of it is withered, the Lord is departed from us. Learn to be more zealous, and God will return and cause you to flourish again; for when God looks upon a people, it is with them as with the earth in spring time; and when he departs from them, they are as withered trees in winter. Where now is the zeal of former times, the communion of saints, the warming and whetting of one another by mutual exhortations? where is the boldness for the Lord? Those holy prayers, those former times are gone; the light of those times remain, but not the heat.

As also if we look back upon that generation of queen Elizabeth, how are we changed! They were zealous, but here is another generation come in their room, that is dead, and cold, and yet we have their light. But, I beseech you, that you would now begin to stir up yourselves, especially in these times of fasting, when there must be an extraordinary renewing of a man's covenant with God, that you would not now be so cold, and so diluted as you have been; and seeing you have that you would have, and have long desired public days of humiliation, that you would labour to spend them with all care and diligence and quickness of spirit, and to consider that the main work is to be done at home with yourselves; for the end of these days is, that you may be humbled, which you will never be, till you consider your particular sins. Get up early in the morning, for then your spirits are quick, and so you will have a long time before you come to the congregation; and get you all that while alone, and consider your particular sins, and the holy duties you neglect, and renew your repentance, and enter into covenant; and then when you come hither, you shall find the word to have another manner of working upon you than it hath ordinarily.

Use 2. If God be thus ready to punish his own children, and thus sharply, it shows the sin of those that are fearless and careless, which provoketh God exceedingly; " I am very sore displeased with the heathen that are at ease," Zech. i. 15. The heathens had sins enough besides to anger the Lord, yet this sin did it above other sins; and it is not to be wondered at that it should, for it is a rule in philosophy, and most true, that of all things that which provoketh a man most is contempt, insomuch that Aristotle maketh it the only cause of anger, though therein he is deceived, yet it is the main. We sometimes say, "It is a sign of contempt not to answer again;" as when a man is chidden and stricken, to go by, as if he took no notice of it at God's hand, this is contempt. And thus a father, when he is angry with his son, or a master with his servant, how heinously doth he take it! And so God, who now hath discovered his wrath to the whole land, and to every particular man in it, this neglect of him will cause his wrath to wax hot against us. But yet for the land in general we have cause to hope that his wrath doth not so, but that God takes it well at our hands, that we are thus publicly assembled. But let me say this to every particular man, though God spare the kingdom, yet if thou neglect him and be careless, it will go the worse with thee however. In Psa. l. when Asaph had expressed great threatenings in the former verses, he concludes with this, "Consider this, ye that forget God," you that mind him not, "lest I tear you in pieces, and there be none to deliver:" and so in Jer. v. 12—14, because they said "the prophets shall become wind; wherefore thus saith the Lord God, I will make my words in their mouth fire, and the people wood, and it shall devour them." This is the great fault of men, that they are ready to fear things which they should not fear—the creatures, poverty, and discredit; but are backward to fear the Lord.

God says of the church, "Fear none of those things thou shalt suffer," Rev. ii. 12; what all the world fears that do not you fear; fear not the things you shall suffer, those things you ought not to fear; but fear those things you ought to fear: and who is afraid of them, lest he should provoke God in them? And so Christ saith, Fear not men, no, not those that have power of life and death: if we should fear any, it should be them. Remember that was the commendation of Moses, he "feared not the wrath of Pharaoh." When you place your fear thus amiss, it becomes a snare to you; for it makes your hearts busy upon the creature, when they ought to be set upon the Lord; but when your fear is placed upon God, it doth exceedingly help you, nothing more so. To give you an instance or two: you shall find David exceedingly struck with the fear of the Lord, when Ziklag was burned; no accident ever so amazed him: when he fled before Absalom, he bore it much better, yet that fear helped all, for it set him at work to pray. So Jehoshaphat's fear did also help him; when he heard of a great army coming against him, it set him on work to pray, and so turned away the judgment. And therefore things that you so fear, when your fear is placed on God, seldom come to pass, for that sets men on work to prevent them, whereas evil fear brings the thing with it. Saul feared the armies of the Philistines exceedingly, that made him seek to the witch, and this wrought his overthrow which he feared. Jeroboam feared the loss of his kingdom, and that fear made him set up the calves, by which he lost his kingdom indeed. Learn therefore to fear the Lord; nothing brings a judgment so much as the want of fear: security is the next door to a judgment. Lachish was a secure people, and when the army came against them, they and their city fell as figs that are ripe from a tree, so did they fall in their enemies mouths: security is a forerunner to every man's judgment. "To this man will I look," saith God, "even to him that is poor and of a contrite heart, and trembleth at my word," Isa. lxvi. 2: if not, I will neglect him as much as he me; I will have no eye to save him, as he hath no eye to me to cause him to fear and tremble.

But you will say, How may I bring my heart to fear the Lord? I answer, First pray to the Lord to strike your hearts with the fear of him; it is the work of God to bring the fear of himself upon us, for it is he that brings the fear of one man upon another: he brought a fear upon all the nations of the land, when the people of Israel entered Canaan, much more the fear of himself; for the affections are such things as the Lord only can meddle with, and therefore the apostle saith, "For this is the commandment, that we should love one another."

It is the Lord that must put such an affection into you, for his teaching is planting the affections. And so he is said to teach other creatures, that is, to give this or that inclination; and so the Lord is said to fashion the hearts of men, and then they cannot fail to fear him: therefore go to the Lord and say, Lord I am not able to fear thee: and say, Lord, thou hast promised to give the Holy Ghost, who worketh every grace, to those that ask thee. If you would seek him so, and seek him importunately, though you had the proudest, hardest heart of any in the world, he would at length teach you to fear him. "I will put my fear in their hearts, that they shall not depart from me," Jer.xxxii. 40. Thus you see that God takes the doing of this to himself; it must be of his planting, and he hath promised also, you see, to do it.

This is not all, but there is something we must do ourselves. Therefore, observe the Lord's dealing with his; learn to know him in his ways, and that will be a means to cause thee to fear him. If any of his children sin, he never lets them go, for then they would thrive in evil, and prosper in sin; but if they will be meddling, they shall be sure to find some bitterness in the end. When a man's heart is set upon the creatures, there being thorns in them all, if he will grasp too much of them or too hard, he shall find it to his cost. God's children are trained up so, that God will not let them go away with a sin; if they be too idolatrously affected, they shall find a cross in such an idol: you may observe this in Psa. xxx.; there you may see the circle God moves in with his children. David had many afflictions, as appeareth by ver. 5: he cried, and then God returned to him, and joy came. What did David then? "In my prosperity I said, I shall never be moved:" his heart grew wanton, but God would not let him go away so. At ver. 7, he is, you see, in trouble again; "Lord, thou didst hide thy face and I was troubled." Well, David cries again, ver. 8 and 10, and then God turned his mourning into joy again. And this is his usual dealing; you shall find it in all the scriptures: but because we find this his dealing set so close together in this psalm, therefore I name it. Therefore observe the ways of the Lord to you; and they that are not acquainted with these his ways, as yet in themselves, see what he hath done to others in all the world, in our neighbour churches. When he had given a bill of divorce to Israel, yet Judah had not feared: now when God hath struck our neighbour churches, do you think he will take it well, if we be idle spectators? therefore when he hath stricken another place, learn to fear.

Use 3. If God afflict his own children thus sharply, let them that are not his look to themselves; whether they be gross sinners, and profane persons, of whom there is no question; or mere moral men, and formal professors, in whom there is no power of grace. If he be thus hot against his own church, his anger will be seven times hotter against you: it may be longer deferred, as his manner is, yet when he strikes he will strike you in the root, not in the branches; and that so as he will not strike the second time; consider that "he will tear you in pieces," Psa. l. 22. And you that are profane ones, let me say to you, "Do you provoke the Lord to anger? are you stronger than he?" 1 Cor. x. 22. Those that lie in open profaneness, and fight openly against the Lord, and have not so much as a show of turning; those that are outwardly moral, that yet are in health, wealth, and credit in the world, and yet lie in secret sins, it is a sign that God means them no good; he would not let his own ground go so long unploughed.

And let professors, that do not answer their profession in their lives, take heed, for "he that is not with me is against me." It may be thou art no enemy, not very stirring in any evil way, but because thou art not with God in good earnest, because your hearts are not perfect, at the last day you will be found against him. Christ will come against you in good earnest as an enemy; and whereas all your hope is, that God is merciful and Christ is a Saviour, learn to know, that this Jesus, whom you hope to be saved by, will prove the sharpest enemy against you. "Kiss the Son lest he be angry:" the Son may be angry, as he who in Rev. i. hath his "eyes like a flame of fire, and his feet like fine brass," to tread you to powder; he will come against you that are formal. And know, that Jesus Christ is not only a Saviour, but a Lord; that he came into the world to be a Prince; and the government is upon his shoulders: you forget that part of his office, half the end for which

Christ came into the world. And if you would know what kind of governor he is, "I send an angel (that is Christ) before you," saith God, "beware of him, and obey his voice, and provoke him not, for my name is in him," Exod. xxiii. 21. He is of the same spirit and disposition with his Father, and they are both alike affected towards sin; beware of him, he goes along with you, and he will not spare you, for the Lord hath put all the government upon him.

Use 4. Let it not seem strange, that he hath dealt, or should deal thus with his churches abroad. What though the candlestick be removed out of the Palatinate? because they were lukewarm, and fallen from their first love. What if he should do it in France? what if in England? in the Low Countries? should it seem strange to us? It is his manner so to do; he removed Judah and Jerusalem often out of their places. We should not be offended at it if he doth, or if he should do thus with us, as thinking that it is a sign that our religion is not the true religion, and that he doth not love his churches; yes, those he loves most he soonest afflicts, for "judgment must begin at the house of God;" that is, he looks on all the world, as on Europe now, and where he seeth his house is, there he beginneth with them, for he is to use others to afflict them; and therefore he begins with them first. So in Amos iii. 2, "You only have I known of all the families of the earth, therefore will I punish you" soonest and most frequently, though not more deeply than others; for though the church be brought under water, yet she shall rise again. I speak this, because men are apt to be offended at it; and Bellarmine, I remember, makes that an argument, that the romish is the true church, because it has had so many victories against the protestants, and our church hath been ever and anon down; but by that argument the captivity should not have lighted upon Judah, but upon Nebuchadnezzar's people.

The second doctrine was, that THOUGH GOD SEND VERY SHARP AFFLICTIONS UPON HIS OWN PEOPLE, YET THEREIN HIS KINDNESS AND COMPASSIONS ARE EXCEEDING GREAT TOWARDS THEM. He calls them you see, " my people ;" as if he would have said, You are mine, and I cannot forget you. A man loves that which is his own, much more God, who is all love. And this doctrine had need to be added to the former.

Now the reasons and demonstrations of this are three.

1. Because he is exceedingly slow to afflict, and exceedingly long ere he does begin, therefore he often makes many offers before he does it, as one that could find in his heart not to do it at all. It is said, he " being full of compassion, forgave their iniquity, yea, many a time turned he his anger away," Psa. lxxviii. 38; when his hand was up, and he giving the blow, he called it back again, as one that could not find in his heart to do it; and when he did it, "he did not stir up all his wrath:" he let fall some drops of it, but would not shed the whole shower of it; and he giveth the reason of both, for " they are but flesh." Indeed his primary scope is to show mercy, and that he afflicts, is but upon occasion; and therefore he is provoked, and provoked much before he doth it: as it is natural to the bee to give honey, and it stings only when it is provoked. And this we see to be true by experience, Providence suffers men, and suffers them long; they continue in their sins, and yet mercies are continued, and judgments withheld.

2. God's compassion is shown in sustaining them in

their afflictions, and in helping them in the midst of them. When his people should fall by the sword, and by the flame, &c. it is said they should be "holpen with a little help," Dan. xi. 33, 34; that is, so much as would sustain them, bear them up. The like we have Zech. xiii. 9, " I will bring the third part through the fire, and will refine them as silver is refined;" and they should lose nothing but their dross, as he would sustain them, hold them up. And this he doth by two things; by *moderating their affliction*, and by so *framing and fashioning their hearts*, so as they shall be able to bear them.

He *moderates their affliction;* they are still in measure, and not beyond their strength. Christ saith to the church of Smyrna, "Fear none of those things which thou shalt suffer; behold, the devil shall cast some of you into prison, that ye may be tried, and ye shall have tribulations ten days," Rev. ii. 10. As if he should have said, I will moderate this persecution, and do measure out the time to you,—but ten days and no more, and therefore fear not: so as you shall not have so much as Satan desires, for he would never give over; nor so little as you would have, for then you would not be afflicted at all. If you now ask, What it is to be afflicted in measure? I answer, If afflictions lie so upon his children as to cause them to put forth their hands to wickedness, then it is above measure; but if so as they never fret nor faint under it, it is not. Now God hath promised, that he will so accommodate afflictions, as they shall not work so with his people; " The rod of the wicked shall not rest upon the lot of the righteous, lest he put forth his hand unto iniquity," Psa. cxxv. 3. It shall not be so long as to cause a distemper in the spirit of them, so as they should not carry themselves in a meek manner under it. I do not mean, but that at the first it may cause a bustling in their spirits, as it did in Job, when it grew sharp, and he spake unadvisedly; yet not an obstinate disquiet; he came to himself again. To this purpose let Psalm cxxix. 3, 4, be compared with the former. God there compares the afflicters of his people to ploughers set to plough his ground; (the Babylonians and all the other enemies were but God's ploughers;) now they should not do it, so as to do them any hurt, no more than for his and his churches' advantage: they should not go a foot further, for then God cuts their cords in sunder; and when the traces are cut, then the plough stands still, goes not a jot further, let the horses do what they will.

The second way of sustaining them is, in that he so *fashioneth their hearts*, as they shall be well able to bear it; and then, though it be great, if they have strength to bear it, it is the less. A great burden on a strong man's shoulders, is no more than a small one on a weak man's. We often wonder that God should lay such great afflictions on his children, but we do not see the inward strength and ability they have to bear them.

(1.) Now first he fashioneth their hearts to pray, and not to murmur; and the greatest affliction is as nothing if they can but pray. In Rom. viii. 26, there is one comfort brought in among the rest, that sweeteneth our afflictions, that "the Spirit helpeth our infirmities," and teacheth us to pray.

(2.) He frameth their hearts to repent, and that they should not sin against him; and if sin be not mingled with an affliction, it is not bitter, if a good conscience be joined with it: for it is only heavy, when it falls upon a shoulder out of joint, or upon a sore place; and therefore St. Paul cared not for death or the prison, because he had a clear conscience; all his afflictions were nothing to him, for he bare them with a whole shoulder. Sin wounds the soul, and then affliction dropped in, causeth smart.

(3.) He frames their hearts to patience; and that keeps their spirit whole, so as that they possess their souls, and themselves: as on the contrary, impatience takes the soul off the hinges, puts it out of itself. Whilst a man's spirit is strong and patient, it will bear its infirmities; but when impatient, it will bear nothing. When therefore afflictions are thus mingled with prayers and repentance, and a good conscience and patience, it is easy to bear them; and it is God mingles their cup thus. And as Christ said, " The cup which my Father hath given me, shall I not drink it?" Although the cup be bitter, yet the ingredients he puts in it makes it sweet: God mingles a cup in another manner to them and to others. See how he mingled a cup to Ahithophel; it was no great thing in itself, it was but a disparagement in the rejection of his counsel, yet such an ingredient was put in, such an apprehension by God's providence, (for though God was not the author of it, yet he suffered Satan to do it,) as that it brake his heart, and he hanged himself. See the contrary in David, when Ziklag was burnt, a great and sudden affliction, yet he bare it well, for he had comfort from the Lord; an ingredient with it which encouraged him in God: and so when he fled before Absalom his own son, a great and bitter affliction, yet he bare it with such a mind, as if he had been in his bed asleep, as appears by Psa. iii. which was made upon that occasion, when ten thousand were encamped against him; yet he feared no more, than if he had had never an enemy in the world; " I laid me down and slept," ver. 5.

3. His compassion is shown in bringing them through, and giving them a good issue and comfortable fruit of all; as appears by Zech. xiii. 9. He carried them through the fire, and refined them thereby as gold, led them out, and caused them to lose nothing but their dross; or as the wheat loseth nothing in the winnowing, but the chaff. There is an excellent passage to this purpose in Isa. xxvii. 8. "In measure in the branches thereof thou wilt debate with it," so some read it. God promiseth in the former part that Israel should grow like a fruitful tree, and flourish; and though he afflicted him, yet it should not be so as he afflicted others. Hath he smitten him, as he smote those that smote him? no, he smote them in the root, but him in the branches, so as he should grow the more by it. God compares himself to a man that loppeth his tree, but meddleth not with the root or body of the tree, but with the branches only, and that just so far as is needed; and where they should be cut, and that in season, and at the right time, that it may grow the more; for this is to do it in measure. And this is no more than necessary to make the tree shoot the more; and it would be spoiled, if he did not deal thus with it. Now he smites others at such a time as they are most unfit for it, and that in the root, so that he causeth them to wither. They are losers by it, as appears by that wicked king Joram; "This evil is of the Lord; what should I wait for the Lord any longer?" 2 Kings vi. 33: and by that of Ahaz, "In the time of his distress did he trespass yet more against the Lord," 2 Chron. xxviii. 22, &c.; this was that king Ahaz, this was the end of that affliction.

Object.—But some soul will object, and say, I do not find this fruit of my afflictions.

Answ.—It may be thou doest not for the present; but stay a little till God hath made an end, and thou shalt see that very affliction which thou thoughtest most sharp, and for which thou sawest no reason, and by which for a while you saw you got no good; yet when the Lord hath made an end, and put all together, then, I say, thou shalt find thy worst takings, thy worst condition, profitable and useful to thee. In the time of winter, when the trees wither, an unwise man would wonder to see such a spoil, but when the spring comes, you know the benefit of it; you would not have had such a spring but for such a winter: and so those varieties of afflictions and crosses through which God leads us, those falls, those puttings back, which we think can no way be advantageous to us, they ever in the end will bring forth a spring time; for "all things work together for good." Judge not by one particular, but stay till God hath put all together, and thou shalt see it is for good. Thence it is that St. James would have us, when we fall into divers temptations, to count it exceeding great joy, James i. 2; he doth not say, when you go in step by step, but when you are precipitated, fall suddenly, and are plunged into them, so the word in the original signifieth. And again, not into one, but into all sorts, into divers afflictions at once; affliction in estate, body, wife, children, one upon the neck of another: yet rejoice, and not only so, but be exceeding glad; as glad as a merchant man is to see his ships come from the Indies laden with riches, and full of treasure; so beneficial should they be in the end. Now, except they did always bring home such treasure, and proved not in the issue exceedingly good and profitable, he could not have desired them thus to rejoice.

Now if you ask the reasons why it is so, that God deals thus with his children in afflictions, I answer out of the text.

First, says he, they are "my people;" they are his own, and therefore he is full of tender compassion towards them, as a man is to his own child, because it is his, Hos. xi. 8. Thou art mine, and I cannot deal with thee as with a stranger, for "mine heart is turned within me," as it is there; when it came to the casting away of his child, he cannot do it. So, in 1 Sam. xii. 22; "The Lord will not forsake you," for you are his people. And so also, Micah vii. 18; "Who is a God like unto thee, that pardoneth iniquity, and passeth by the transgression of the remnant of his heritage?"—there lies the reason, they are a remnant, they are chosen out of the rest of the world; and to them he is so merciful, as there is none like unto him, it would make a man stand amazed at it.

They are a "people called by his name." As he hath chosen them to be his, so it is taken notice of that they are his, and he hath owned them; his name is upon them by profession, and therefore he will spare them, for his name's sake; because of them that stand by and take notice of them: for if he should deal hardly with them, none would serve him; for when servants are hardly dealt with, who will serve such masters? And this argument Moses uses, Numb. xiv. 13—19; Lord spare them, says he, and if it be, but for thy name's sake, for what will all the nations say? that either thou art such a God as art unkind, and wouldest not save them, or a weak God, and couldest not.

But you will say, We see the contrary by daily experience, we see great and sore afflictions befal

God's people; yea, it may be some of his people will say, they have felt and tasted of great afflictions.

I answer, you may mistake in afflictions, they are not always such afflictions as they seem to be ; for as we say of the sun,—" The sun keeps his light even in eclipses, firm and clear ;" so those afflictions which you think great, are often nothing at all in themselves, they only seem so to us. So the apostle, " As sorrowful, yet always rejoicing; as having nothing, and yet possessing all things," 2 Cor. vi. 10 ; all was nothing to Paul ; for affliction lies only in the apprehension, and many of those grievous afflictions and tortures which martyrs and the children of God endured, though to us they seem great, yet I am persuaded were as nothing to many of them.

But thou wilt say, This is not my case ; I feel, I am sure, the sting of it.

I answer, first, that God lays it not on thee, till thou hast need. The physician knows the body of the patient better than himself; and the soul hath more intricate diseases than the body, and He sees thy secret pride, security, &c. it may be when thou seest them not, as Hezekiah did not ; so that when thou seest no reason for such a sharp affliction as sharp physic for thee, he doth ; and he does not administer it but when there is need

And secondly, he doth not go a jot beyond thy need; and this will appear by the opening of two excellent scripture similitudes, for all the wits in the world cannot find out better expressions than the sacred word hath, if we had eyes to see the glory of them :—
" Doth the ploughman plough all day to sow? doth he open and break the clods of his ground? when he hath made plain the face thereof, doth he not cast

abroad the fitches, and scatter the cummin, and cast in the wheat, and the barley and rye? for his God doth instruct him to discretion," Isa. xxviii. 24—26. The husbandman, he tells you, ploughs not but where he means to sow, and to have an harvest, and the plough goes no longer than till the clods be broken, and says he, God hath given him this discretion; and therefore shall not God have the same, and use the same himself? Dost thou think that thou art ploughed longer than thou needest? it is but till the clods, thy stiff spirit, be broken. And whereas thou mayest think thy heart soft enough, it may be so for some grace, but God hath seeds of all sorts to cast in, the wheat and the rye; and that ground which is soft enough for one, is not for another. And when it comes to harvest, to some maturity, he hath to thresh it with divers kinds of instruments, which is the second similitude, ver. 27, 28. "The fitches are not threshed with a threshing instrument, neither is a cart wheel turned about upon the cummin, but the fitches are beaten out with a staff, and the cummin with a rod; but bread corn is bruised, because he will not ever be threshing it." So God beholdeth every man's strength, and knows what affliction is most suitable for him; he finds out a fit instrument for every grain; his end is but to drive thee out of the husk of thy easily besetting sin. Some lusts sit more close to the heart than others: and as the wheat and the husk are closer together than in other grains, therefore the wheel goes over it; and when it is threshed enough, and God hath unloosed the heart and the sin, the husk and the wheat, he doth it no longer. Now, says he, "this is from the Lord, who is wonderful in counsel, and excellent in working;" and therefore when you see an husbandman do so with his ground and grain, you judge him a wise man in doing so, so also is God wise therein.

But you will say, For all these good words and setting it forth thus, we are sure, and see, and feel by experience, that the saints always fare as ill as the worst: when general afflictions come, plague, sword, or captivity, they are swept away by these, as well as others; and what afflictions are there which go through the sons of men, that fall not upon the saints as well as upon others?

For answer: It is true, those deluges of afflictions which overwhelm whole countries take away one as well as another, yet there is a difference: as in Jer. xxiv. all were carried into the same captivity by the same king, but yet they were carried in divers baskets, the bad in one basket, the good in another; which shows the condition of the one was different from the other. 1. The Lord knows the good figs, his eyes are upon them for good, to see that no hurt should befal them, that was hurt indeed. 2. He did but send them into captivity, as one is sent on an errand; but the others are led as a condemned man to the jail. 3. He would bring them again, when they had done the business for which they were sent, when they had humbled themselves and sanctified his name more—many the like ends the Lord hath: but the others he utterly destroyed, and they never returned.

But, some will say, (for the manner of man is to complain,) The afflictions that I endure are of an extraordinary nature; never any was so afflicted as I, there is a peculiarity in mine, and it is not one but many, and these for a long time have lain upon me.

I answer, it is true, they are often of an extraordinary nature, and there is good reason for it; for a small affliction would not bring thee home to God.

It is not a little head-ache, a scratch with a pin that drives a man to the physician, but such a disease as a man apprehends death in, makes him seek out for help. And the reason why these afflictions are many, is, because thou hast many diseases to be healed, lusts of divers sorts, and thou must have diversity of afflictions applied to them. And again, if God should not change afflictions, thy affliction would grow familiar; and as physic when it is made familiar to the body works not, so would not those afflictions. And they are also often long, because some sins stick close, and are not easily got off; the stain in some sinks deeper, and requires a great deal of scouring. "Many shall fall by the sword, and by flame," &c. Dan. xi. 33. Their trials were of many kinds, and long, that they might be made white; into which yet men would not fall nor continue in, if they would be scoured and made white sooner. I have dwelt longer upon this and the opening of it, because either it hath or will be of much use one day to many of us: and seeing we know not what we are reserved for, it is good to treasure up these things, that we may know the ways of God beforehand, and so bear what comes the better; for it is ignorance that makes afflictions so unsupportable when they come.

Use 1. Learn hence not to be discouraged whatsoever thy case be, whether thou hast been afflicted in name by reproaches, so as thou thinkest thou shalt never get thy credit again; or in body by diseases, that thou shalt never have thy health again; or in soul by doubts, that thou art in such an estate that thou shalt never be raised again. Remember the exceeding great kindness of the Lord, and know whatsoever thine afflictions be, he is able easily to scatter them. This I speak, because as men in prosperity think it will always continue, and "to morrow will be as to day, and much more abundant;" so in affliction, that it will never be otherwise. What unfaithfulness is this! are not all times in God's hands? as David says, Psalm xxxi. 15. That God that alters the weather, and that turns the winter into summer. It is a storm now, and half an hour after the sun shines; all in the weather: so such alterations God is able to make in men's estates. And comfort thyself with this—it shall lie no longer on thee than there is need; the plaster shall not lie a moment longer than while the sore is healing. If it were sooner healed, it would fall off sooner: but then it shall fall off at once; though "weeping may endure for a night, but joy cometh in the morning;" because the anger of God never lasteth but for a while; and the reason is given, Micah vii. 18, "he delighteth in mercy." Take him always when he is angry with his children, and there is but a short brunt of it, his constant course is otherwise; "he delighteth in mercy." Now that which a man delights in he will be long doing, he can hardly be taken off from it; as if it grieved him to do otherwise. When therefore it is long, it is when thy heart is harder than ordinary; for some are more stubborn than others. Ah, but thou wilt say, This of mine is a great affliction, and I know not how it should be helped, unless the Lord should work miracles. It may be it is so; and indeed when God will send an affliction, all the world cannot keep it off. In Zech. i. there were four horns that beset the children of Israel to afflict them, so that which way soever they went and would have fled, one would have met them, whether to the east or to the west, &c.; no way was left to escape, no evasion; for when God will afflict, he will afflict, and there shall be no door to go out at; else it were not an affliction. But yet what do these horns serve for but to push them home to the Lord? And though a man cannot escape them, yet there is this comfort, that though those horns be as strong as the horns of an unicorn, so that all the world cannot knock them off, yet when they have pushed them to the Lord, then the prophet saw four carpenters; and wherefore came those carpenters? to knock off every horn, and to cast them out, so that every nation was frayed away that was against Judah; neither the Assyrian, nor Babylon, nor any of them were left. So when God will afflict a man, nothing can hinder him; so also when the Lord will scatter the affliction again, and will raise a man, nothing can hinder it, he will do it be it ever so great. Be not discouraged then: what though the storm grow great and violent? one word of his mouth will allay and still both storms and winds, as in Mark iv. 39. Take the most grievous disease that thou hast long lain under, and from which thou thinkest thou shalt never recover, yet one word will rebuke it: take the worst and most bitter and most powerful enemy of the church, such as Haman, if God speak but a word to him, as he did to Laban, "Hurt not this man," he cannot hurt thee; one word of the Lord Jesus tames them all; only bring faith with thee. In the great storm, Christ saith to his disciples, "Why are ye so fearful? how is it that ye have no faith?" Mark iv. 40, 41, when they were so exceedingly troubled; as if he had said, It is not the greatness of this storm that causes this fear, but the littleness of your faith. So when all the people murmured at the Red Sea, what was the reason that Moses was quiet all that while when they murmured? " Stand still," saith he, " and see the salvation of the Lord." The reason of the difference was, Moses believed, they did not. So that the trouble comes not from the greatness of the affliction, but the littleness of your faith. When therefore afflictions come, be not discouraged; lose not yourselves, but possess yourselves with patience: keep this as a sure conclusion against all objections, that God will be merciful to his people.

Use 2. Is the Lord then so full of pity and kindness to his own people? Learn thou to come to the Lord, when you have offended him. If indeed God had such a hard heart as would never relent, then when you had sinned, you might go somewhere else for comfort; but now come again unto the Lord, as being assured of good success. This use we see made of it by Samuel in the like case to the people of Israel, 1 Sam. xii. When the people had committed a great sin, wherein, as he told them, they had not only cast away him, but the Lord; and God had declared his wrath against them in storms from heaven, in the time of the latter harvest: yet at verse 20, saith Samuel, "Fear not: ye have done all this wickedness, yet turn not aside from following the Lord;" and he giveth two reasons: 1. Because all other things they would go to, would not profit them, they were vain; 2. Because the Lord will not forsake his people, for his great name's sake, because it hath pleased Him to make you his people. As if he had said, I would not have you lessen the sin, or seek out excuses,—as indeed that is our fault in such cases; no, that is not the way; you have committed a monstrous transgression, yet forsake not the Lord. Samuel said this, because that which often keeps men off from the Lord is discouragement. The main thing that keeps many off, is, men do not think God so ready to receive and pardon them. Now therefore, says Samuel, you are his people, and the Lord cannot forsake his own. Let a man have a child of his own, even when it is young and troublesome, and may act unpleasantly, yet because it is his own, his affections will not depart from it; yea his affections will hold on, because it is his own, although when it is grown up, it provoke him a hundred times. Now if they should ask how it comes to pass that they are his, Samuel tells them, "Because it pleased God to make you his people;" there is no other reason can be given for it. So that if any of the children of God, looking upon all the world lying in wickedness, should ask the reason, Why should I be in this good condition rather than they, there is none other than, It pleased God to make you so. God loves for no merits, which should teach us to look out of ourselves, less into our hearts in this case, and more to the attributes of God. God says, in Jer. iii., it is true indeed, that if you come to any man in the world when his wife hath played the harlot, will he receive her again? no; a man's heart in this case cannot relent, he hath not mercy enough, his heart is too narrow; "but thou hast played the harlot with many lovers, yet return again to me, saith the Lord;" for look, how much larger God's heart is than a man's, so much larger are his mercies.

Use 3. If God be thus exceeding merciful and pitiful, this should lead men to repentance: there is that in the thing that should lead you, so Romans ii. 4: when God either expresseth his mercies toward us by his behaviour and merciful dealings with us, or causeth his ministers to offer mercies unto us, it should lead to repentance. It hath indeed a contrary effect almost in all the world; for whom do not God's mercies lead from him, rather than to him? But take heed lest you turn the grace of God into wantonness, which men ordinarily do. The more favour, the more means they have enjoyed, the more wanton they grow, that is the more bold, losing their respect for God: even as a child is apt to do when his father carries himself kindly towards him; he cannot bear it; he hath not the discretion to consider, that it should lead him to obedience, but he grows bold and wanton. And you should also make this use of mercies, that the meditations of them should stir up your hearts to a more kindly sorrow for your sins; to think that you have deserved to be cut off long ago, and that you have committed such sins, for which many are in hell long since. God expects this at your hands; and let us make this use of it in these days of humiliation, the main work whereof is to humble yourselves. And we are to labour to humble you, not only by denouncing God's judgments, but by expressions of his mercies also.

There is a double manner of observing a fast; one wholly public, which should be from morning till night in public by the whole land, that all together might confess and humble themselves for the sins of it; which is more extraordinary. But secondly, as for these days which are kept from week to week, it is well ordered, that the time is so limited for public exercises, as that there is time left for private: for the business of particular humiliation goes forward better then, and public exercises tend but to that end,—and what is the means unless the end be attained? that is, that every man should mourn apart. So Zech. xii. 12—14, when it was a business of mourning, every family did it apart, and the wives apart. The wife and the husband are the nearest, and if any should be together, one would think they should; and yet they must be then apart: and the reason is, because nothing humbleth so much as particular sins, those wound the heart, which in public are not so much confessed, but in general only. But when you are every one in private, then you may consider what your lusts, and your actions have been, and the circumstances of them; then you may search your hearts and ways, look back and reflect upon yourselves.

Some of you, it may be, will say, I know not how to spend my time in private, when I am from the house of God. But consider, hast thou not committed many sins? Call them to mind: canst thou not speak and confess them, and say, Lord, I confess I have fallen back into this sin again and again? But further: when you have done this, seek reconciliation, and beg it earnestly, which the heart will do when it is touched with the sense of sin; and the enumeration of them will work your hearts to it, when you see the multitudes, the circumstances, the aggravations of them. And because this is the greatest of all your requests, therefore you must be the most earnest in it; because God doth purposely often withhold assurance, to teach men what it is to be reconciled to him. Fasting serves to help your prayers, that they may be the more earnest. Again: renew your covenant also; consider what sins you are most inclined to, and what occasions draw you most to those sins, and vow against them. Consider what good duties you have most slighted, and what your hearts are most apt to fail in, and promise better obedience. Further: not only make a promise, but labour to bring your hearts to be willing in good earnest to leave those sins and to perform those duties; for when the heart is strongly biassed any way, it is no easy matter to get an inward willingness; you must therefore have much reasoning with your hearts to bring them to it. Lastly: when they are brought into a good temper, they are easily subject to be distempered again. Our affections shoot too far into worldly business; our love, our fear, our grief are subject to be too much fixed on earthly things, and it is not easy to bring the soul back again; you must therefore take a great deal of pains with your hearts.

That which is said of ministers, " fullers of men's souls," every man is now to be himself, to wash out the stains of his heart, and to make his soul whiter, as it is, Dan. xi. 35; and that will move God either not to bring afflictions, or to remove them. Therefore "cleanse yourselves from all filthiness of flesh and spirit," and know that to get stains of a deep die out will cost a great deal of pains. If you do the work yourselves thus, and plough your own hearts, God will not need do it by afflictions; therefore do it, and give not over till you have done it, and have brought your hearts to be thoroughly humbled for sin, for that is a great means to do it. What else is the meaning of that in James iv. 8, " Cleanse your hands, ye sinners; and purify your hearts, ye double-minded?" But how should we do it? some may say; " Be afflicted, and mourn, and weep; let your laughter be turned to mourning." Be content to sit alone, get out of company, and not take your former liberties; and mourn and humble yourselves. And do it constantly; for it is not bowing down the head for a day, which God regards; but let sorrow abide in your hearts: it is continuance that God regards. Do it, and do it to purpose; for the want of this, is the reason of the coldness and remissness in our profession, namely, that we are not thoroughly and constantly humbled: humility is the ground and promotes the growth of every grace. Seeds sown in a heart broken in pieces, thrives and prospers; but instructions falling upon a heart not broken, will bring forth no fruit. If you were humbled, we should find wonderful fruit of our ministry. Do this therefore but one day, and you will be the fitter for it the next. Sorrow should be as a spring that runs along constantly from day to day. The sorrows of many are but as land-floods. And take heed, how the continuance of this duty from week to week, thus makes you slacken your course therein; suffer not your hands to faint. When these duties are new, you are apt to do much; but when a while continued, to be careless in them. And let not any man complain that he loseth a day's work; for is there any work so necessary as the salvation of the soul? Neither complain, that a day's study is lost; for is there any excellency to be compared to the image of God stamped on the heart?

Use 4. We are hence to be exhorted to choose the Lord for our God, when we hear he is so merciful a God; for no man ever served the Lord, but he first made choice of him to be his Master. Every man when he comes to years of discretion, and to be master of himself, adviseth with himself what course he should take. Now all the saints of God have made this distinct choice—we will serve the Lord, and go to no other. Moses, when there stood before him the pleasures of Egypt on the one hand, and God and his people with their afflictions on the other, chose the latter before the former. It is said of him, "By faith Moses, when he was come to years, refused to be called the son of Pharaoh's daughter; choosing rather to suffer affliction with the people of God, than to enjoy the pleasures of sin for a season," Heb. xi. 24, 25. So David saith he did; " I have chosen the way of truth : thy judgments have I laid before me," Psa. cxix. 30. So Joshua said, " As for me and my house we will serve the Lord."

Now, I exhort you, that seeing you are to make some choice, that seeing God is such a God, so exceeding merciful, that you would make this choice—let him be your God : for what moves a man to make choice of one course of life rather than another? the ground of it is some happiness that he seeks. When men consider what makes most for their happiness, that they will choose. Now if men were persuaded that to choose God were the best way for happiness, they could not but choose him; and surely if God be so exceedingly kind and merciful a God, their chief happiness cannot but be found in him alone. And surely there is no husband nor friend so loving as he; no father so kind as he, so tender hearted; he goes beyond all the sons of men, for love and tenderness and kindness : for if there be any kindness in any man or woman, the Lord hath put it in him. The natural affection in parents is not as a drop to the ocean, nor as a beam to the sun, compared to what is in him; and if the kindness in them be an excellency, then surely it is in him. And if the Lord hath commanded us to be amiable, and full of bowels of mercy and goodness, and easy to be entreated, as being a part of his image, and that holy frame of heart which ought to be in us, is it not then much more in himself?

But that I may not urge a bare exhortation without some reason, consider how merciful the Lord hath been to us, and how gracious he is to them that make choice of him: for first he giveth them the comfort of his presence—and there is no comfort like that. For joy and comfort are nothing else but the agreeableness of a thing to a man's mind. Now, there is nothing that better agreeth with man's mind than the presence and face of God; for lusts and pleasures are the diseases of the soul, and the pleasures that agree to them are the destruction of it. Besides, when thou art reconciled to him, thou art out of all debt and danger; he will set thy soul at rest, that was restless before. Moreover, when thou hast the Lord to be thy God, thou hast one to whom thou mayest go, and unbosom thyself, to advise withal, when thou canst not go to any creature in the world; one thou mayest fetch comfort from, when thou seest no comfort any where else: thou mayest run to him as to a refuge, when thou art overwhelmed with oppositions, slanders, and ill reports. And besides all this, and the glory which we shall have in heaven, consider what there is that thy heart can desire, that he will not do for thee. If thou hast any business to do, God will do it better for thee, than thou canst for thyself: the Lord works all our works in us, and for us, Isa. xxvi. 12. Art thou a scholar, and hast studies to bring to perfection? or a tradesman, and hast enterprises to bring to pass? or art thou in straits?—he will be entreated of thee to do all for thee, if thou go to him; and he will bring it better to pass than thou canst, with all thy policy. Again, art thou fallen into poverty, into sickness, into disgrace?—thou shalt find him exceedingly kind. When thou art sick, he will be careful and watchful over thee: this David acknowledges; " I will be glad and rejoice in thy mercy; for thou hast considered my trouble, and hast known my soul in adversities," Psa. xxxi. 7. When others overlook and forget thee in adversity, as the butler did Joseph, he will not, but will take care of thee. Again, if thou art persecuted, and hast enemies to deal with, (as who hath not that liveth godly? so that you say as David said of himself, " My soul is among lions,") yet thou shalt find God stand by thee, as he did by Saint Paul, to deliver thee out of the mouth of those lions: thou shalt find him to be as a rock, as a place of defence, to shield thee against them and all their incursions, so that all their plots and malice shall not hurt thee. David had often trial of God in this. Again, if thou dost want any thing, he hath promised to grant whatsoever thou shalt ask in faith. But if thou shalt say, I provoke him day by day; yet know that he is exceedingly kind, and will pass by many infirmities, for he knows whereof we are made: one ill turn causeth not him, as it doth men, to forget what was done before. The Lord keepeth for us " the sure mercies of David;" that is, such mercies as the Lord showed David, and not to him only, but to all his posterity; so that he will not only be a God to thee, whilst living, but, when thou art dead, to thy seed also. Such a God you shall find him; therefore take him for your God and for your husband. If men knew him, they would choose him; as Saint Paul said to Agrippa, " I would that thou wert altogether as I;" that is, if thou didst know Christ as I do, and his service, thou wouldst not be half a christian, but one altogether: do but try; if thou likest not his service, thou mayest leave it. But the saints, who have had experience of both conditions, hold an argument of God's kindness unto all his people; and this also should move us to choose him for our Master.

Use 5. As the preceding use was to those who are without, to choose the Lord, this use is to all those that are already in the covenant, to exhort them to confirm themselves in their choice, to be more and more well persuaded of him, that so they may love the Lord more and more, and cleave faster to him. One that is married may love her husband well, and yet by seeing increasingly the excellences that are in her husband, she may be more confirmed in her choice. In all afflictions labour to think well of God, and ill of yourselves. This was the praise of David, he always laboured to extol God in all, and still held this conclusion, "yet God is good to Israel." We are apt to fail much this way, we are ready to think that God deals hardly with us and his people; but we must learn to correct this error, and to have a good opinion of him, to labour to extol his mercy. But this we cannot do, till we see these two things: 1. God's exceeding great kindness; 2. Our exceeding rebellions. You look only on God's dealings, and so are ready to think that God hath dealt hardly with you, but never think how abominable your conduct has been to him. But, however, learn to think, that he is a God full of compassion, that he is exceedingly kind, even in your worst condition; and that you have deserved worse at his hands. Labour to think of this for yourselves, and also for the church. God hath been merciful to his church in all ages, and is so still. So Moses saith, "Lord, thou hast been our dwelling place," that is, a house for the church to dwell in safely, "in all generations." From Abraham's time to the time they were in Egypt, he was their habitation; and so in the wilderness; and so in all the times under the judges; and so to our times. Look on the church when it was in the worst condition. Take the church of God, even when it was thought to be cut off, as in the great massacre in France; yet then was the Lord a habitation to it; a company was kept alive, that grew greater than the former. So in queen Mary's time, God suffered the storm to overtake the church a little, but it was soon blown over; God was a habitation to keep off the storm from destroying his people. And so he hath been, and will yet be. So he hath been found to our church above all the rest; for our nation hath been like Gideon's fleece; when all others about us have been wet and wallowing in blood, we have been dry. Therefore labour to see how good God is, and how base we are, and take heed of abusing his kindness, lest he make this nation wet with blood, when all others shall be dry, and we come to have war, when all the rest have peace. The way to have his favours continued, is to remember them, and to humble ourselves before him in thankfulness. Thus much of this doctrine.

The third doctrine was—THE LORD'S NAME IS CALLED UPON HIS PEOPLE; that is, they are called by his name.

For the opening of this point, we must know, that it is the Lord that putteth his name upon them: for who durst take this honour, but those upon whom the Lord himself pleaseth to bestow it? This is no small thing; where God puts his name, it brings something with it. So that it is not an empty title, but there is a reality in it; for where God gives his name to any man or people, there he bestows himself, and all that he hath is theirs, because they are God's, 1 Cor. iii. 21—23. As a husband when he bestows his name upon his wife, then he also giveth himself to her. Now, in the scripture the Lord's name, and the Lord himself, are put one for another; so that it is no small privilege to have the Lord's name called upon us.

And to open this further, let us consider, who they are that are called by another's name amongst men. Wives are called by the name of their husbands; children by the name of their parents; temples are called by their names to whom they are dedicated; and they that addict themselves to some man to follow his opinion, are called by his name, as the Platonists, Aristotelians, Ramists, &c. from their masters.

In the same respects, those that are called by God's name are such as are married to him, and that are born of him, for they are his children, and all such are the temples dedicated to his service. Also all such as are resolved to follow him, as Joshua was, who said, "As for me and my house we will serve the Lord;" and as Jacob was, "The Lord shall be my God." All these are called by the name of the Lord, and the Lord is called by their names; for he is called "The God of Abraham, Isaac, and Jacob," &c. It seems that there is, as it were, a certain union between them, a mutual agreement and relation, as there is between a husband and a wife, a father and a son; so if thou art married to Christ, and he hath changed thy heart, and begotten thee anew by his word, and thou art dedicated to his service as his temple, then thou art called by his name.

And the only reason of this is, because he hath chosen thee,—there is none other. When he cast his eyes upon all the earth, he chose thee out, to have his name called on thee; as it is said of the temple at Jerusalem, that he chose that place rather than any other, to put his name there. And there is the same reason why his name is called upon a whole church;

as when he looked on Europe, he chose out the reformed churches to put his name there; and where the Lord puts his name, there he dwells: so that the one is put for the other, either to say, he chose a place to dwell in, or that his name is called upon it.

There are two places where God dwelleth; " Thus saith the high and lofty One that inhabiteth eternity, whose name is Holy; I dwell in the high and holy place, with him also that is of a contrite and humble spirit," Isa. lvii. 15. The highest heavens and the lowest hearts are God's chief dwelling-places. He hath indeed other places, he dwelleth elsewhere; but in these two he manifesteth a peculiarity of his presence, and that peculiarity is of the presence of his grace and comfort; for he saith in the same verse, " To revive the spirit of the humble, and to revive the heart of the contrite ones." He reveals himself and his secrets to these, which are hid from all the rest, and he fills their hearts with joy and comfort.

Use 1. If we be such as bear the name of God, then let us learn to be obedient unto him, to give up ourselves unto him; for so much is intimated by this, that we " are called by his name." We are therefore said in scripture to be baptized into the name of Jesus Christ; that is, we do by our baptism profess thus much, that we give ourselves to his service; for to bear his name is to bear our own names no more, that is, our own natures no more. A man that is called by the name of the Lord is no more his own man; as a man that giveth himself to serve another, inasmuch as he serveth himself, so much he wrongeth that man. And the reason why a wife leaves her own name, is to show that she is to give up herself to the obedience of her husband; she is not mistress of herself, not free; she depends on her husband as the ivy on the tree; she hath no root of her own to rest on, but dependeth on him. So we, having taken the name of the Lord upon us, must remember that we are no longer free; we leave our own names; we must have no more root in ourselves, but in the Lord; we must have no will of our own, his will must be ours. Ye, therefore, that bear the name of the Lord, let it not be in profession only, but do that thing which the name requireth, that is, follow no more yourselves, but follow God. A woman bears the name of her father, but when she is married, as she leaves that name, so she leaves father and mother to cleave to her husband. If her parents command one thing, and her husband another, she leaves her father and mother, and cleaves to her husband. As leaving father and mother implies leaving to bear affection to them, in comparison to her husband, so must you do for Christ, as you have it in Luke xiv. 26. If thou wouldest be joined to the Lord, thou must be divorced from all things else in the world; from every thing that is very near and dear to thee. Father and mother, sons and daughters are dear, but you must renounce them all, if need be, for Christ's sake, or you cannot be his disciples: yea, he that is married to the Lord, must hate and deny his own soul; when his own soul desires one thing, and Christ another, he must deny it, and be divorced from himself, and take no root from himself, but from the Lord, because he only is able to sustain him. Wives are not bound to destroy themselves for their husbands; but this bond is nearer, therefore, this near conjunction between man and wife is made but as a shadow of that between Christ and his church, who is flesh of his flesh, and bone of his bone, Eph. v. 30—32. And, as for this cause they leave father and mother, as the apostle says, ver. 31, so for this cause must we leave all to cleave to Christ, and be subject to him, as ver. 24; that is, our will must be subject to the Lord's. As if thou hast such a journey to go, say, But what says my Husband to it? Thus St. James teaches us to speak, "We will go into such a city, if the Lord will," James iv. 13, 15. So in other business, say, If the Lord will, to whom I am married, I will do it, not else. And you have reason for it, because Christ loves us as his spouse and body. By this union we are one flesh with him, yea, one spirit; and "no man ever yet hated his own flesh," saith the apostle. Though a man have all the imperfections or wounds in his body that may be, yet he hates not his own flesh, but laboureth partly to cover those wounds and imperfections, and to heal them, if he can; for it is his own body: so doth the Lord love you, if you have taken him to be your Husband; you have reason therefore never to forsake him. And if any should object, and say, I am a sinful wretch, an unfit match for him; consider that yet being his, he will cover your imperfections with his righteousness, as a man covers his sores from the view of others; he will wash you from your corruptions. As if a man have a sore arm, he doth not only cover it, but also washes it, and heals it, because it is a member of his. So, saith the apostle, Christ cleanseth his church with the "washing of water;" and this he calleth "a great mystery." As if he had said, Great things are now revealed therein to you, and worth your considering: why therefore should we not give up ourselves to him? A wife may object against her husband, and say, Another one's husband is more wise, more kind; but thou canst say nothing against him. Consider this, and let it not only be a notion in your heads, but let it sink down into your hearts; and let the name of the Lord not only be upon you, but also in you. As we have it in Exod. xxiii. 21, spoken of the angel that went with the church in the wilderness; " My name is in him." My name is not only *upon* him, so that he is not only called my angel, but my name is also *in* him; that is, he is so affected as I am, he hates sin as I do, and therefore will punish it in you; and loves what is good as I do. So let the Lord's name be in you; that is, labour to be of the same mind and disposition that God is of, to have a heart after his heart, to be affected as he is. Labour to be thus minded, and you shall be the glory of the Lord, as the wife is the glory of her husband, as she is called, 1 Cor. xi. 7; because when she behaves herself wisely and virtuously, those that see her do commend her husband: therefore so behave thyself in the world, so show thyself like thy husband, that thou be his glory; show forth the praises of Christ, as the apostle has it in 1 Pet. ii. 9. A man must so behave himself that the image of God may appear in him, and then he shall be his glory; as a wife when she carries herself as the image of her husband, so that his wisdom and virtues appear in her, then she is his glory. Consider this seriously; you are called by God's name; if you make this but an empty title, then you shall have but an empty benefit by it: but if in earnest you cleave to him, and follow him, then he is yours and you are his, and all that is in himself is yours.

Use 2. If at any time you sin against God, this should be a great motive to humble yourselves the more, that you have sinned against Him whose name you bear, to whom thou hast given up thy name, and made a vow and promise to obey. Thus learn to aggravate your sin, for it doth aggravate it. There is a double humiliation; one comes from self love, and that sometimes makes way for grace, but is not grace. But there is another that comes from a tender affection and love to God and Christ; for when a man loves any one, he desires to please him, and therefore when he displeaseth him, it grieveth him: and this is such a humiliation, as is required of us on these days of fasting, therefore labour to work your hearts to this.

Now there is nothing that will kindly work our hearts to be humble more than love. Nearness will surely make us love God; for why doth the wife love the husband, and the husband the wife, but because they are near one to another? Now when the name of the Lord is called upon us, it is an argument that we are near unto him; therefore let that soften thy heart, that thou shouldest carry thyself unworthy of this nearness. It was that which smote the heart of David, when he considered how kind and loving the Lord had been to him. The Lord himself when he comes to humble his people, taketh this course with them, to tell them of the nearness that is between them and himself, as is plain in Jer. ii. 2, 3. Thus saith the Lord, "I remember thee," that is, put thee in mind of, "the kindness of thy youth," that is, which I showed thee in thy youth, "the love of thine espousals." Now when we see the Lord take this course, we should take the same. When he would humble David, he sent Nathan to humble him, this was one part of his message, to tell him of God's kindness to him; "Thus saith the Lord, I anointed thee king over Israel, and I delivered thee out of the hand of Saul," 2 Sam. xii. 7, 8. And this, doubtless, was the chief cause that made him confess and say, "I have sinned against the Lord," as it is in

Psa. li. 4; he repeats "against thee" twice: there lies the emphasis, "I have sinned against thee," "against thee have I sinned;" that wounded him in a peculiar manner that there was so great a nearness between the Lord and him.

When a man commits a sin, there are two things to be considered in it; first, in that he sins against the law of God, and so he sees a great obliquity in sin; when he looks on sin and the straight law of God, he sees a deformity in it: but this alone doth not humble us in that kindly manner; this will make us vile in our own eyes, this will make us to see a wonderful deformity in ourselves. But now there is another thing to be seen in sin, and that is, the person against whom we commit it, and that is the Lord: and sin so looked upon comes to have another relation put upon it, not only as an obliquity and deformity, but as an injury, as a rebellion, an unkindness, recompensing evil for good. The first way sin is considered as an obliquity from a straight rule; but in the latter as against the person of God, as against thy Husband.

Now therefore to humble thee, do thus; go through all the particular dealings of God with thee, remember all the special kindnesses of the Lord, his keeping thee from thy youth, his many deliverances, how many special kindnesses he hath done thee, recount his mercies; and when thou hast done this, then go to thy sins, and say, These are not only transgressions against God's straight law, but also, they are unkindnesses and injuries against his person. And add to all this, the consideration of the patience of God,— Though I have played the wretch and been false, as never any have been, yet he hath been patient, and is so kind, as he bids me yet to return. This will cause thy heart to melt towards him: labour to do this more and more.

There is an exercise of humiliation which is done after the manner spoken of, by seeing the Lord's kindness to thee, and thy injury against him, and comparing the one with the other. But thou wilt say, I would fain do it, but I cannot; my heart is hard, and I cannot get it thus melted. Therefore I say, exercise thyself to this. The reason men's hearts are thus hard, is, because they are idle, not willing to recount God's mercies to them. Say not thy heart is hard, but thou art sluggish: this therefore you ought to do, especially at this time. In Lev. xxiii. 29, there was a time set apart for the Israelites, for the performance of this duty of humiliation, and it was to be their exercise that day; they were then to labour to afflict their souls; such as did not, were to be " cut off from among his people." And this consideration, that we are called by the name of the Lord, is a means to do it.

But you will say, I have done this, and yet my heart is hard still.

It may be so indeed, and your heart not softened; but yet this I say, first, for thy comfort, that if thou continue doing this, the Lord accepteth it; but if thou doest it not, thy blood shall be upon thine own head. We only require that thou shouldest labour to do it, and the Lord will accept it, though thou art not able to soften thine heart. Secondly, know for thy comfort also, that God will join with thee, if thou labour thus with thy heart, and send the Spirit of humiliation on thee. As the disciples, though they rowed all night, yet Christ came at the last; so though thou toilest many days, and makest no proficiency, as thou thinkest, yet know that God at length will come and help thee; and because he hath commanded thee to do this, he will not suffer you to be doing that always in vain, which he commandeth; and therefore he will come. But that you may have the more ground for this, remember that you have many promises made of God's help; as in Luke xi. 13, "If ye then, being evil, know how to give good gifts unto your children, how much more shall your heavenly Father give the Holy Spirit to them that ask him?" You will never, of yourselves, be able to soften your hearts; but continue knocking, and the Lord will give you the Holy Ghost, though you be but strangers. So that every man may come to God and say, Lord, thou hast made such a promise, thou canst not go from thy word, and therefore deny me not: be earnest with God, and he cannot deny thee. The woman of Canaan was not a jewess, yet she having this ground, that he was the Messiah, she would not be put off; therefore do thou so, and thou shalt in the end find that thy heart is softened. And the longer thou waitest, the greater measure thou shalt have of the Spirit; and when thou hast him, he shall humble thy heart, as in Zech. xii. 10, "I will pour upon the house of David, and upon the inhabitants of Jerusalem, the Spirit of grace and of supplications: and they shall look upon me whom they have pierced, and they shall mourn for him, as one mourneth for his only son." The people of Israel were here exhorted to mourn, and to separate themselves, and to do it every family apart. The business was the same that you are to do every fast day. Now, says God, if you seek me aright, you must have the Spirit; and says God, I will do my part, "I will pour on you the Spirit of bowels," for so the word may be translated. The meaning of it is, that when the Spirit of God is upon you thus, you will be tenderly affected to the Lord, even as a mother toward her child. Then, saith he, " They shall look upon me whom they have pierced, and they shall mourn for him, as one mourneth for his only son, and be in bitterness for him;" that is, you shall then remember your rebellions, and the remembrance of them shall be bitter to your souls, as bitter things are to your taste. So it was with Josiah; the reason why his heart melted, and he wept when he heard the book of the law read, was because he had the Spirit of bowels, which every one of us should have. So Job; " Now I have seen thee, I abhor myself," Job xlii. 5, 6; he was not thus before. He was a holy man, but this was a new work; for says he, " I have heard of thee by the hearing of the ear, but now mine eye seeth thee." He was enlightened anew, as it were; the Spirit shined into his heart with a new light: I have been in a mist all this while, in comparison; but now mine eye hath seen God, and I have an experimental feeling of him, now I abhor myself. It is a hard thing to abhor a man's self thus, which then a man doth, when the Spirit of God with a new light, enableth a man to see God's love and kindness, and his own unkindness in their true colours.

Use 3. If the Lord's name be called upon us, we should learn hence to keep his name fair, to keep it pure and unspotted; as it was said of St. Paul, he was "a chosen vessel to bear God's name;" and therefore it behoves them to take heed how it be polluted by them, or they give occasion that it be blasphemed; for the evil committed by you reflects upon the name of the Lord. A small thing is a great matter in you; one fly corrupts a box of ointment, but many flies in a barrel of pitch or tar are counted nothing: so, many sins in a wicked man, redound not so much to the dishonour of God's name, as one in a saint. When a saint doth a thing that is uncomely, he polluteth the name of the Lord; not that it can be polluted in itself, but it seems so to other men. Before men are regenerate, their sins are as blots upon a tablet, before a picture be drawn upon it, which are not regarded by any; but after it is drawn, the least blot is seen by every one: so it is when men are strangers to God; the sins which they commit, reflect not to the dishonour of God; but when God's image is renewed in a man, then these sins are more taken notice of, and cause the name of God to be blasphemed by his enemies.

Use 4. This should teach us, not to be ashamed of God and the profession of his name: for the Lord will not be ashamed of us, as he shows he is not, when he is willing to put his name upon us: and shall we be ashamed of him? It is an unreasonable and an unseemly thing for a child to be ashamed of his father, or for a wife to be ashamed of her husband, and so also for us to be ashamed of the Lord, whose name we bear.

This is the rather to be spoken of, because it is a fault very common amongst us, that we do not take notice of. But the most will say, we are not ashamed of religion, for we account it rather a glory to be accounted christians.

Give me leave to examine you by two questions: —First. Are you not ashamed of the strictest ways of religion? There is a common course of religion, that you need not be ashamed of, because all are for it, and commend it; but yet there are some special acts of religion that men cast shame upon: such was that act of David, when he danced before the ark, which seemed absurd in Michal's eyes for a king to do; yet he said, "I will be yet more vile." Some of the ways of God give a more peculiar distaste to wicked men; and there is a shame cast upon the power of religion, by reason that the multitude goeth another way. Now, shame is cast upon that which is singular; as in any thing, let the multitude have ever so ill-favoured a fashion, it is no shame; whereas, if a few others wear a garment far more comely, but different from the fashion, yet it would be a shame to them. So it is here: there is shame cast upon holiness and sincerity, because the multitude is not holy; for holy men are like the gleanings after the harvest, or like the grapes after the vintage, exceeding few, and not enough to bring godliness into fashion. Therefore if thou wouldest know whether thou art ashamed of God or no, try whether or not thou art ashamed of any of the peculiar acts of religion, upon which shame is usually cast among men.

The second question I would ask is this—Are you ashamed of God, or any task or duty, or his people, among those where the shame will do you some hurt? Consider whether you are not ashamed of religion among sinners. It is an expression put in for some cause in Mark viii. 38, "Whosoever shall be ashamed of me and of my words in this adulterous and sinful generation, of him shall the Son of man be ashamed." As if he would have said, It may be you would not be ashamed of me among saints; but he that is ashamed of me amongst the worst of men, and in a dangerous time, in a time when it is ignominious to be a christian, as it was then, of that man will I be ashamed in the day of the resurrection. You must therefore try yourselves, by what you do before wicked men, and what you do before great men, when it is some loss to you to profess Christ, or any truth of his; and know that this is not a small matter. We must profess Christ in our times, we must make the word of God the rule of our lives. Perhaps we think, that so long as our hearts are right, and so that we run not out into evil ways with others, the matter of profession is but a small concern; that it is but as the leaves of godliness: if God have the fruit, what need we care for the leaves? But remember that text in Rom. x. 10; "With the heart man believeth unto righteousness; and with the mouth confession is made unto salvation." This will damn many of us, the want of professing Christ, as well as the greatest sins. The scripture is peremptory; we must profess God's name at all times, even then when we shall do it with the danger of our lives. You know that Daniel did so, at the peril of his life; and it was not a needless matter, but it was in a matter that concerned his life. But that you may do this the more willingly, consider why men are ashamed of this profession. Why? because men do speak evil of you: but is this a good reason? No; for they do so out of their ignorance, as it is in 1 Pet. iv. 4. "Wherein they think it strange that ye run not with them to the same excess of riot, speaking evil of you." But if they knew the ground of your actions, they would not speak evil of you. They see your actions, but your rules and principles that you go by in these actions, they know not; and therefore they speak evil of you. And shall we be discouraged for this? What if a geometrician should be drawing lines and figures, and there should come in a countryman, and seeing him, should laugh at him; would the geometrician leave off his art for this laughing? surely not; for he knows he laughs at him out of ignorance, not knowing the art and the grounds thereof; and is it not as great a folly for us to be ashamed of godliness, because men that understand it not, speak evil of it? surely it is. And therefore remember David's two reasons, when he did that act for which he was reviled by his wife. "I did it for the Lord that chose me:" as if he should have said, The Lord deserved it; he loved and chose me, therefore I did it. So this is thy case: the Lord hath chosen thee, when he hath passed by many thousands of others; therefore do it for the Lord. And another reason of David's was, It makes for my honour in the eyes of those that are good, 2 Sam. vi. 22. Men think it brings no honour, because they shall not get any credit by it amongst men; but know thus much, when men shrink from God, then God makes true that rule, "They that despise me shall be lightly esteemed." He that hath made a profession of godliness, and afterward falls away, God never suffers such a one to escape, but he punisheth him one way or other. Therefore Moses exhorteth the people in Deut. iv. 6, to keep God's statutes and to do them; for "this is your wisdom and your understanding in the sight of the nations." Now why should you be backward to bear the shame that the world casteth upon you? Doth not God observe all, and look on with approbation? Doth not God tell the church of Ephesus, in Rev. ii. 2, "I know thy works, and thy labour, and thy patience," &c. When any man at any time casteth shame upon you for religion, it is a persecution which God will record; as Luther said, when any spake evil against him, "This will be accounted on my reckoning at the last day:" that speech is to be considered and weighed by us all. "I know thy patience;" therefore be not ashamed, but be bold in the profession and fear of God, doing those things that are glorious in the eyes of God and of those men that judge of things aright.

Use 5. If the name of the Lord be called upon us, this should comfort us concerning ourselves, and concerning the church of God; for where God's name is called upon any church, any nation, or any man, you may be sure he will defend them; for he is engaged so to do, that his name may not be polluted: for the Lord is the worse spoken of, when his people suffer. Therefore thou, whosoever thou art, rich or poor, be confident, God will defend thee in all thy sufferings. A man will not suffer his wife to be wronged; for, saith he, she is my wife; he accounts himself wronged, when any injury is done to her: so God accounteth himself injured, when any wrong is done to those on whom his name is called. Although, saith the Lord, they may seem to be helpless, notwithstanding this, " fear not, I will create a cloud by day, and a flaming fire by night," Isa. iv. 5; that is, though there be no means, yet I will work without means. " I will create them," make them of nothing: I will be both their direction and protection. For the cloud by day and the fire by night, have reference to that cloud which went before the children of Israel in the wilderness, that led them in the way, and kept them from the heat of the sun. " For upon all the glory shall be a defence;" that is, the churches, though they seem ever so base, yet they are glorious; for therefore they are called glorious. And not only upon one man or two, but upon " all the glory;" that is, every man in the church; upon " all the glory" shall be a defence.

But then if this objection come, Why! do we not see them afflicted? do they not often suffer a storm? are they not often scorched with the heat of reproach? Therefore, the Lord saith, as they have divers persecutions, so will I have divers means of help: " And there shall be a tabernacle for a shadow in the day time from the heat, and for a place of refuge ;" like the cities of refuge whither they fled that were pursued by the avengers of blood. " And for a covert from storm and from rain," Isa. iv. 6. The saints, in a storm of persecution or any calamity, are as a man under a shelter; whereas all others are in the midst of the storm. Therefore be you assured, the Lord will not forsake his own people; they are as " the apple of his eye:" a man may bear much, but he will not suffer you to touch the apple of his eye; so God will suffer much, but he will be avenged on them that wrong his people. Thus much for this doctrine.

Sec. II. ON HUMILIATION.

---

2 Chron. vii. 14.

IF MY PEOPLE, WHICH ARE CALLED BY MY NAME, SHALL HUMBLE THEMSELVES.

We are now come to the conditions upon which mercy and forgiveness are here promised, whereof the first you see is humiliation; "If my people shall humble themselves." In the handling of which I will proceed two ways;

First. Negatively—That without humiliation, and unless men do humble themselves, they can have no interest in these promises.

Second. Affirmatively—That if they do humble themselves, then God will be merciful to them, and forgive their sins.

For the handling of the first, I raise this doctrine out of the words: THAT WITHOUT HUMILIATION NO MAN SHALL OBTAIN MERCY. We see that God suspendeth mercy upon it here, as that without which no mercy can be expected; which therefore must needs be thought a matter of great consequence, and the more largely to be insisted upon.

I express the doctrine in a more large and general word, humiliation; which contains in it, as well humiliation *passive*, or being humbled; as humiliation *active*, (as for the sake of distinction I call them,) whereby we humble ourselves. This is the main thing intended in the text, explicitly and directly, which also in the prosecution of this point I mainly intend. Yet

I shut up both together, in the negative part of this discourse; because they are, though in themselves distinct, yet always conjoined in their working; and the latter doth always presuppose the former, and doth necessarily imply it here; for no man did ever come to humble himself, that was not first humbled. This negative part of excluding men from mercy without both these, being also alike common to both; it being alike true, that no man ever did attain mercy, that was not first humbled, and who did not humble himself: so that in this negative part they agree and concur.

Again, though that affirmative part mentioned is proper to that humiliation active, (the promises of interest in mercy being made to them that humble themselves, and not to all that are humbled; there being many that are much humbled who yet do not obtain mercy,) yet I join both together in this first part; chiefly, because as they are conjoined in their working, so they must necessarily be in the explication of them; for we cannot come distinctly to know and find out what it is to humble ourselves, which is the thing I principally aim at, without knowing what it is to be humbled; the one beginning where the other ends: the one being a preparative to the other. Therefore that we may see how far the one and the other goes, and how they are distinguished, we will include both in this first doctrine.

Now in handling this doctrine we will do two things:—

I. Show that men must be humbled, and humble themselves, ere they can come to have an interest in these promises.

II. We will show what it is to humble a man's self, and to be humbled.

I. For the first, this passage alone is sufficient

ground. God would not have put in such a condition in vain, if it might have been spared in any: his plan is, to humble men, that they might be brought to humble themselves. And, to omit all other instances, we have the seals of all the three Persons in the Godhead to this method.

When God would draw Adam and Eve to seek the promise of mercy, he first expostulates the matter with them, to humble them for their sin; and then lets fall the promise of the Messiah.

And again, Jesus Christ, the second Person, in his first sermons in preaching the gospel, as in Luke iv. 18, shows his approbation of this method, in that he makes this his first subject of his first sermon, as appears by the text he takes to preach the gospel: but to whom? to those that are humble; "The Spirit of the Lord is upon me, because he hath anointed me to preach the gospel to the poor, to heal the brokenhearted."

And Christ foretold that the Holy Ghost, the third Person, when he was come, would observe the same order in working upon men's hearts by the ministry of the apostles; "He shall convince the world of sin," John xvi. 8, for humiliation, that is his first work: then " of righteousness," for justification: lastly, " of judgment;" that is, that sanctification which persons justified are to have wrought in them. We come now to the explication and reasons of this point, which are,

1. To show the necessity of this humiliation.

2. The order of it, as it is here placed first.

1. For the first, it is true indeed, that the Lord might bring men home to him without this humiliation. He could do as he did at the first creation, say no more but, "Let there be light," and there

would be light, and that without any of this thunder: he might say, Let there be grace, and there would be grace: he could come in the still voice, without rending the rocks, and say no more but, Open ye everlasting doors, lift up your heads, ye gates, and they would be open: but though he might have brought the children of Israel out of Egypt into the land of Canaan, without leading them through the wilderness, yet his good pleasure was thereby rather "to humble them and prove them;" so it is here.

I. The reasons of this necessity may be drawn from the relation and respect which this humiliation hath both to the other conditions that follow, and all that is promised here in the text; unto which we will fit the reasons that follow.

(1.) Without this, men will not seek out for, and come unto Christ: they will not seek his face, that is, his person. The law is our schoolmaster to bring us to Christ, by humbling us. Men will not come unto him unless they are driven; men will not seek him unless they are convinced they are lost; men will not receive him unless they are first humbled. The poor receive the gospel, the poor in spirit.

(2.) It is necessary in respect of receiving and seeking for mercy, and pardon, and forgiveness; which is the main thing here promised, "I will forgive their sins;" for until then our propounding pardon and the promises of it, and inviting men to come in, would be all but lost labour: for until then, men will give us that answer, and the promises the same entertainment, which those did that were invited to the marriage feast, Matt. xxii. 5, 6—"they made light of it." And so we find by experience, that when we preach the great things of the gospel, as justification and remission of sins, men account them as small things, and set light by them; and the reason is, because they are not humbled. Men do not prize Christ and the promise of pardon by him, (as manna was not prized by the Israelites,) nor his righteousness, by which they are to be justified. A man, perhaps, would be content to have Christ's righteousness, as a bridge to go upon to heaven; but he will not prize it as Paul did, who was ambitious of nothing so much as to be "found in Christ, not having his own righteousness, but that which is by faith;" accounting all things in himself, and out of himself, dross and dung in comparison with it. But a man unhumbled will not set this high prize upon it; and God will not have his jewels, much less Christ and pardon of sin, cast away at random to those who do not value them. But when a man sees the badness of his nature, the multitudes of his particular sins, and sees that in his heart which he never thought had been there, and stands amazed at them, then to have such a righteousness as shall perfectly cover all these sins, this he will think a great matter. So it was to St. Paul, when he saw himself the greatest of sinners. And when a man thus sees his particular sores and diseases, and something in Christ's righteousness to answer them all,—as Christ's patience to answer his impatience, Christ's love to stand for his hatred, Christ's holiness of nature to cover his uncleanness,—he will then begin to esteem every jewel in that cabinet; for he knows he could not spare one part of that righteousness. He sees a glorious righteousness to clothe and cover his nakedness from top to toe; and this makes him prize it, and every part of it, which a man unhumbled will not do. And as a natural man does not esteem the imputed righteousness of Christ, so also inherent righteousness from him, whereby he may be enabled to turn from his evil ways. But when a man sees and knows what a heart he hath, how false, how full of sins, and empty of grace, and what strong lusts are there, then when he finds the contrary graces wrought in him, he prizeth them highly, and Christ for them, because they are the precious gifts of Christ; for he knows and acknowledges they are the sole work of Christ, because in his own nature dwelleth no good thing. And why else doth God suffer his people to fall into sin after conversion, and into a variety of temptations, but that they might be still more humbled, and so know the worth of Christ?

(3.) It is required that men should be humbled, because else they will not actually turn from their evil ways, nor be obedient to Christ in all things in their lives. An unbroken heart is like an untamed horse, that will not endure the bridle, and be guided by it; like an untamed heifer that will not go with the yoke. God may command such a man what he will, but he will do what he pleases: but when the heart is broken and once humbled, then, as St. Paul tremblingly said, he will say also, "Lord, what wilt thou have me do?" Acts ix. 6. I will do what thou wilt, yea, and suffer what thou wilt; call me to suffer for thee. If this question had been asked St. Paul before he was thus humbled, he would have given another answer. God may bid us do what he will, but we as stubborn servants will do what we think good. We are proud and unbroken, and pride is the cause of all disobedience; and therefore it is said, that high thoughts must be cast down, that exalt themselves against the knowledge of God, before every thought can be brought to the obedience of Christ, 2 Cor. x. 5. They exalt themselves against the knowledge of God and his will; for when his will is known, the heart still yields not. When the Lord commands any thing, as to take heed of evil company, to have a care of their speech, whilst men are unhumbled, they are ready to expostulate the matter, and in the end will do nothing at all: but when a man is humbled, and the high thoughts cast down, then he brings every thought and affection, that exalted itself before, into the obedience of Christ. And as all disobedience is from pride and stubbornness of the will, so all obedience is from humility. When the heart is humbled, it is made pliable to God; "To this man will I look, that is of a contrite spirit, and trembleth at my word," Isa. lxvi. 2. They are both there joined; that is, when he heareth any command from God, he is afraid to break it, afraid of admitting the very occasions of sinning. A man that hath been burnt with fire dares not easily meddle with it again. The reason is, it makes a man choose the Lord freely for his gracious Lord, and from thence follows kind obedience to him. He that hath made the choice himself will serve, else not; but he will condemn himself, that he should make a choice so unsuitable to him. It also teacheth a man to set a high price upon Christ, and forgiveness of sins, as you hear; and that will set all his desires at work, and cause him to refuse no obedience whether active or passive. For what is the reason men obey their lusts, but because they prize pleasures, have a high esteem of honours, &c.; and the same effect will the prizing of Christ have in thee, to do any thing for him, so that thou shalt not count thy life dear for him.

(4.) They would not do all this constantly and for ever, if they were to come to Christ and be obedient only for a while, as John's hearers and Herod were;

they would return unto their vomit again, and not stay with him, if they were not humbled; they might come in, as those hearers signified by the stony ground did, who received the seed with joy, or as those of whom it is said, Christ would not commit himself to them; but stay with him men will not, unless they are humbled. For unless a man be brought to part with all for Christ, and to sell all, he will in the end repent of his bargain: if there be a reservation of any thing, the time will come when he will go back, and start aside like a broken bow; and until a man is thoroughly humbled, he will not be brought to part with all for Christ. He only that is humbled, is the merchant-like minded man, who sells all he hath, and goes away rejoicing; is glad at the heart that he hath Christ, though with the loss of the whole world. He is willing to take Christ upon all conditions, with losses and crosses, and to deny himself in every thing; for he knows the bitterness of sin, and so sets such a price upon Christ, as though the bargain were to make again, he would do as he had done. But what the other hath done in a fit, he repents of afterwards, and therefore true repentance, which godly sorrow and true humiliation worketh, is called "repentance not to be repented of," 2 Cor. vii. 10. Other sorrow than godly may work a repentance, but it is such as men afterwards repent of. Men are soon weary of the yoke of Christ, because they have not felt how grievous the yoke of sin and Satan is; but to one who hath felt the burden of sin the yoke of Christ is easy and sweet.

(5.) The last reason hath relation to the last thing here promised,—taking away the judgments and healing the land. God would not have the praise of his judgments and of his mercy in taking them away, unless men were humbled; for if when God did afflict men, he should restore them again without this humiliation, they would think that God wronged them before, and now did but right them. But when God hath humbled them so far, that they acknowledge his justice in afflicting them, and their own desert to be utterly destroyed, and confess that it is his mere mercy they are not consumed, and humble themselves under his mighty hand, now if the judgment be taken off, and his wrath blown over, then they give him the praise of his mercy and judgments. —Thus you see why of necessity it is required.

2. Now let us see the reason of the order of it, why it is thus required in the first place: it is the first condition here. There is something in the order, and to be said by way of reason for it; and the reason in general is, because nothing is acceptable to God, till the heart is humbled: you may pray, which is another condition, and you may hear, &c. but all you do is but lost labour, unless it come from a broken heart.

(1.) For that is alone a fit sacrifice for God, without which act no sacrifice is accepted. This you may see: "Thou desirest not sacrifice; else would I give it: thou delightest not in burnt offering. The sacrifices of God are a broken spirit; a broken and a contrite heart, O God, thou wilt not despise," Psa. li. 16, 17. David knew that till his heart was broken, all his good deeds and all holy duties would have been in vain, and it is as if David should have said, Lord, before I was thus humbled, and my heart thus broken, (as in the beginning of the psalm he had expressed that it was,) thou didst desire no sacrifice of me, nor wouldst have delighted in burnt offerings from me; but the sacrifices of God are a broken spirit, and other duties are only accepted as they come from it. This is the main sacrifice, and without it, nothing is acceptable; unless it be laid upon this low altar which sanctifies the sacrifice.

(2.) As it is only a fit sacrifice for God, so this only makes us fit priests to God; and before we are fit to offer a sacrifice acceptable, we must be priests; and we become not priests to God till we have offered ourselves first to God as a sacrifice, 2 Cor. viii. 5; and that we are not, till we ourselves are slain, and broken, and so made a sacrifice.

(3.) Nothing is accepted, till the Holy Ghost dwells in the heart; and until a man is humbled, the Spirit of God dwells not in his heart: and therefore what he doth till then savours not of the Spirit, but of a carnal heart, and so is not acceptable. Till a man is humbled, he keeps the door shut upon the Lord and his Spirit. There is one within, his heart is full already; he dwells in his own heart himself; therefore it is said in Isa. lvii. 15, That God dwells in a contrite heart; that is, in it alone; for there is only room for him to do what he will in all the chambers of it.

(4.) Until a man is obedient in all things, nothing he doth is acceptable: he that turns his ear from the law, his prayer is abominable. Now, one that is not thoroughly humbled may be obedient in many things; he may pray, &c. but yet he will have by-ways of his own; he hath not fully renounced himself, that is, not humbled: now, unless a man's obedience be general, nothing is acceptable.

II. And so we come to the second thing propounded—what this humiliation is; and herein our main inquiry is after that which is mainly intended in the text—what it is to humble a man's self. But because the finding of it out depends upon the other also, we will with it show also what it is to be humbled, that so we may the better know the true humiliation required of us; and for the finding out of this, we will first set before you the examples of those who have humbled themselves, and have been humbled in scripture, and from thence gather what it is.

For this you shall find Manasseh, in 2 Chron. xxxiii. 12, in his affliction humbling himself greatly, and the Lord was intreated of him. Likewise we have that humiliation of St. Paul, where we find him trembling and astonished, saying, "Lord, what wilt thou have me do?" Acts ix. 6. See another example in Acts ii. 37, of those who were pricked in their hearts, crying out, "What shall we do to be saved?" And so of the jailer, who came trembling and astonished, and would have killed himself, Acts xvi. 27, 29; and likewise of the prodigal, which though a parable, yet sets forth to us this condition of a soul humbled, of whom it is said, that "no man gave unto him," and that "he came to himself," &c. Luke xv.

Out of all these we gather those two main parts of humiliation mentioned: humiliation *passive*, and *active*. The first whereof makes way for the second, unto which no promise is made, and which may be found in an unregenerate man; the second, which is a fruit of sanctification, which is meant here, and unto which the promise is made. These go both together in the godly; and he that hath the second never wants the first in some measure more or less, though many have the first that have not the second.

Now the first is nothing else but a sense of sin, and God's wrath for it; expressed to us in those former examples, by being pricked in the heart, it being a wandering of the heart and spirit. Unto which is joined trembling fear, with considering and coming to a man's self, as we have it in the parable.

This passive, legal humiliation stands in these particulars.

A *sensibleness of sin*. Before, a man is as one that is in a dead sleep: what is done to him he feels not, and what is said he hears not; he is sensible of nothing. But this is the awakening of a man to be sensible of sin; so as now he is wounded, now he is smitten with it, now he feels it. So the jailer, as the foundation of the prison was shaken, his heart was also, and he had an earthquake within, as well as one without; and his awaking out of sleep was a resemblance of his awakened heart.

This humiliation *makes a man fearful of his state*; whereas before he was bold; and others that are not humbled go on boldly and are punished, as it is said of the fool in Prov. xxii. 23.

It makes a man *consider his state*, which he never did before; as the prodigal came to himself, that is, entered into a serious consideration of his state. Before, a man thought himself in a good state, and little imagined he was in the gall of bitterness; but this work shows him his poverty, and that he is altogether naked, and that he hath nothing to sustain him, as the prodigal saw he had no worth at all in him.

And this first work of humiliation is wrought by the law and the curse thereof; which says in his hearing, " Cursed is every one that continueth not in all things written in the law to do them." By the law, which is the rule of righteousness, whereof all particular rules are branches; and by the threatenings thereof, which are all branches of that great curse,

The one being as the lightning to discover sin, the other like the thunder-bolt that strikes the heart with fear of God's judgments: the one is like the indictment, the other as the sentence of the judge. I put both these together, because both go to humble a man. The law is like the taskmasters of Egypt, that commanded the Israelites to do the work, but gave them no straw; so the law tells us, that this and this is to be done, and binds us to do it, but gives us no strength, and so thereby discovers our sinfulness and inability to any good: and then, as the task-masters beat them that failed of their tale, so comes the curse, and strikes them dead that continue not in all things to do the law; and these two put together work this legal humiliation. Neither by the law is meant only those ten commandments spoken in Horeb, but together with the explanation of them, as we find them expounded in the prophets and the whole scriptures: so that by the law is meant that rectitude which the whole scriptures require. Now, therefore, when the scriptures are laid to our hearts, the rectitude of the scriptures is compared with the crookedness of our hearts and lives, and thereby we come to see that the least sin is forbidden, and that the least duty must not be omitted, and that we must give an account for every idle word, and every lustful thought and motion in the heart; as St. Paul, when humbled, saw lust to be sin; and then we come to see withal the curse due to the least; this humbleth a man.

And unto this is further required the help of the Spirit joining therewith, without which the law doth not humble a man. He enlighteneth a man to see his bondage and slavery to sin and Satan, and his subjection to God's wrath. He not only shows a man his bondage, but he makes him believe it: for there must be a faith to humble, as well as to comfort; whereas, we set light by the threatenings, and believe them not; for would the swearer swear if he believed that threatening, "The Lord will not hold him guiltless that taketh his name in vain?" When therefore the Spirit enlighteneth a man to see his sins, and makes him believe the threatenings denounced against them, then a man is humbled, and not before.

And yet, though these threatenings are propounded by the word, and made effectual by the Spirit, yet usually some affliction puts life into them; as we see in Manasseh, and also in St. Paul, who was first struck off his horse to the ground; and in the jailer, who thought verily all his prisoners gone, for whom his own life must have been answerable, so that he would have killed himself. Sometimes a real affliction, sometimes an imaginary one, an apprehension of judgment, shame, poverty, misery, doth God use to put life into the threatenings, and they put life into the law; and then the law is brought home to the conscience, and so sin is brought to light. For when men are sensible of miseries, then they are often brought to inquiry into the law of God to find what should be the cause of it; and when the law is brought home to the conscience, then sin is made alive. St. Paul says, "Sin appears to be sin," Rom. vii. 13, which before was as colours in the dark; "but when the commandment came, sin revived, and I died," says Paul there; that is, he apprehended himself a dead man, in which is a discovery of sin, and our subjection to death for it; wherein do consist those two parts of this former humiliation, which makes way for the second humiliation. Thus you see, what it is to be humbled.

Now we come to the next point—What it is to humble a man's self: which begins when the other ends; for then a man looks out for the remedy, as those who cried out, "What shall we do to be saved?" which is the second thing to be observed in these examples. After the wounding of their hearts, they made an inquiry what to do to be saved. For those that belong to God's election go yet further: there is another kind of evangelical humiliation wrought in them, which is a fruit of sanctification. For in one whom God means to save, when he is come to this, the Lord sends the Spirit of adoption into his heart, the "Spirit of grace," as Zechariah calls him, which gives him some secret hope, he shall be received to mercy, if he will come in; which is a work of faith in some degree begun; and then says the soul with itself, I will go and humble myself; I will go home to God, and change my course, and give up myself to him and serve him. And this we shall find in the examples mentioned before, especially of the prodigal: he came to this conclusion, If I stay here, I die for hunger; but in my father's house there is bread enough. Here was hope, which bred this resolution—I will go home, and "say to my father, I have sinned against heaven and before thee," Luke xv. 18. Here was that true humiliation we speak of. So Manasseh humbled himself greatly because he hoped for mercy; for a man comes not to this active humiliation wherein he kindly humbleth himself, unless he hath hope of mercy; and the beginning of faith is with a hope of mercy, which sets a man at work to go to God, and say, Lord, I have committed such and such sins, but I will return to them no more; I am worthy of nothing.

Now there are four several pairs of ingredients that have influence into this second kind of humiliation, to cause us to humble ourselves.

First pair. A hope of mercy, as well as a sense of misery; that whereas before we did look upon God as a severe Judge; we now look on him as one willing to receive us. Both are requisite. Sense of misery only brings a man to himself, as the prodigal first is said to come to himself; but hope of mercy joined with it drives a man home to God, as it did also him: without which, sense of misery drives us from the Lord; but hope of mercy being added to it, causeth this active humiliation we speak of, whereby we say, I will go and humble myself.

Second pair. A sense of our own emptiness, together with an apprehension of that all-sufficiency that there is in God. These we may see in the prodigal, when he said, I shall starve and die, if I stay here; but "in my father's house is bread enough." He looked to that all-sufficient fulness which was in God to supply his wants. The creature, whilst it findeth anything in itself, will stand upon its own foundation, and not be humbled, but when it finds nothing in itself but emptiness, then it beginneth to seek out for a foundation; which seeing to be in God alone, it goes out to him; for men will not be drawn off from themselves, till they see another foundation to rest upon.

Third pair. There must be a sense of a man's own sinfulness, and of the righteousness of the Lord Jesus; and so a light comes in that discovereth both. Thus when St. Paul was humbled, there was a light shone about him, which was an outward symbol of that new light which shone within him, of Christ, and his own sinfulness.

Fourth pair. A sense of the love of God and Christ, joined with a sense of man's own unkindness unto God. By this we look upon sins as injuries done to God, and an unkindness shown to him.

And now let us see the difference between these two works or parts of humiliation, that we may further understand what it is to humble ourselves.

1. They differ in the matter they are conversant about; in that first, a man is humbled properly only for the punishment; a man indeed is humbled for sin, yet principally as it hath relation to punishment; it is guilt works on him. He is not humbled for sin, as it is contrary to God, and his holiness, but as contrary to himself and his own good. And thus we are not humbled, till we come to love God, and to have a light discovering the holiness and purity of his nature, which one that is savingly humbled hath wrought in him.

2. They differ in the grounds and principles whence they arise. The first ariseth from self love, and is but a work of nature; though thus far a work of God, to stir up self-love by the sense of misery, and to awaken it; but so as any unreasonable creature if in danger, useth to be sensible of it: and what wonder then is it for a man, when he begins to have some sense of hell and death let into his conscience, to be wounded and apprehensive of it! But the other ariseth from the love of God kindled in the heart by hope of grace and mercy.

3. They differ in the instrumental causes that work them. The one is wrought by the spirit of bondage, by enlightening a man merely to see his bondage, and the soul is as one that is in bondage, fearing God as a Master; and he hath no further light than

thus to see God as a Judge: but this other is wrought by the Spirit of adoption making the gospel also effectual, discovering God as a Father.

4. They differ in their effects. The one driveth a man from God, but the other causeth a man to go to God and to seek Christ; it works that affection to Christ which the church in the Canticles had to him, who would not give over seeking him, till she had found him whom her soul loved. As a stone hath no rest till it be on its own centre, so, though there be twenty obstacles in the way, the soul thus humbled hath no rest but in God; and therefore gives not over seeking him, though it hath ever so many denials. Again, the first breeds death, a deadness and listlessness; it makes a man as a log that moves not to God in prayer. So it wrought in Nabal and Ahithophel; it breeds such discouragement as often ends in death. Of worldly sorrow (and such is all sorrow whereof God is not the end) cometh death: but when it is right and true and kindly sorrow for sin, it doth that which an affection would do, it quickeneth him to do that which he ought to do. Fear, when it is right, thus worketh, and so all other affections, which were put into the soul for that end, that it might be stirred up by them to that which it should for God and its own good; and therefore this affection of sorrow for sin, when it is right, quickens a man to seek out to God.

5. The first breeds a fierceness and turbulency in a man's spirit; as we often see in men whose consciences are awakened to see their sins; they are fiercer than they were before, for guilt of sin vexeth their spirits: and where there is no sense of mercy from God, there is none to men; for he that is broken for sin spends his anger upon himself, frets

chiefly for his own vileness and unworthiness; and the peace of God, which his heart hath a sense of, makes his spirit gentle, and peaceable, and easy to be entreated and persuaded: bring him scripture, and a child may lead and persuade him. The rough ways are made smooth, the rough and froward dispositions of the heart, and every mountain-like affection cast down, as it is said they were by John the Baptist's ministry, who came to humble and prepare men for Christ.

6. They differ in their continuance. The former alone proves but a passion, and it comes but from flesh; so as all the fruits of flesh are, it is but as the flower of the grass, of the same fading nature as the root is from whence it comes; though it comes like a violent torrent into the heart, and swells above the banks, yet it is but as a land-flood: but this latter is as a constant river that hath a spring, which though it keeps within the banks, and doth not overflow so much as the other, yet it runs constantly, and the further it runs, the greater it grows.

Once more, I will give you also some properties of that humiliation to which the promise is here made, by which it may be yet further known and distinguished.

We will take those fruits of it we find in the text. It will make a man *pray*, and *seek God's face*, and *turn from his evil ways:* it hath always these as the consequences of it.

To *pray*. Judas was humbled, but he had no mind to pray, nor an ability to pray; the spirit of prayer went not with it: but he that hath that true humiliation, is able to pour forth his soul to God. And indeed prayer is not the work of the memory and understanding, but the proper work of a broken heart.

Again, *to seek God's face.* This true humiliation cuts a man off from his own root and foundation, and causeth him to seek the Lord alone; which seeking useth to be expressed in prayer. That other will cause a man to seek mercy, but this to seek God's face; that is, if they have his favour, it is enough; they seek God as sequestered from all things else: though such a soul had assurance of being freed from hell, it would not content him, unless he saw God's face.

That which Absalom counterfeited, as knowing it to be a true strain of a loving and humbled child to a father, when he had his life given him, though, banished from the court, "Let me see my father's face, though he kill me," is in an humbled soul in truth towards God. Others, as God says in Hosea vii. 14, "They have not cried unto me with their heart, when they howled upon their beds."

True humiliation causeth a man *to turn from his evil ways:* the other makes a man but give them over for a time, whilst he is sick of them; and then he returns again, as a dog to his vomit. It is said, "Amon humbled not himself as Manasseh his father had humbled himself, but trespassed more and more," 2 Chron. xxxiii. 23; which implies, that when a man is humbled as he should be, he transgresseth no more as he had done; and Manasseh did so humble himself, that he transgressed no more. It will make him become stronger against that sin he hath transgressed in; as a bone that hath been broken is stronger when it is right set again; he especially humbleth himself for and turns from his beloved sin, and with that from all the rest.

Another property is, it makes a man cleave fast to Christ, and so draw nigh to him in all the duties of obedience, to obey him constantly, generally and thoroughly. Men may have light wounds made in their hearts which do not drive them to the Great Physician, which awakeneth men a little, but they fall asleep again; but when God humbleth a man so as to save him, he so fastens the apprehension of his misery upon him, as to bring him home to Christ; he sets on the avenger of blood to pursue him to the utmost, and not for a mile or two, but to follow him till he be driven into the city of refuge. There is a humiliation which hath not this effect and consequence, and therefore I mention it as a property of the true; and this because of a defect that is in it; in which respect, though it come near the true, yet it differs from it; which is in the event seen in this, that the true humiliation causeth to come to Christ, and to cleave to him without separation.

That you may therefore see the difference between one and the other, and wherein that other is defective, mark how that which is true works this in one, who yet is not quite cut off, but hangs as it were by a thread, there being some secret fibre, some veins and strings that are not cut in pieces, which keep life in the old man, and a man remaineth still upon his old stock, and so long Christ comes not into the heart; nor until a man sees he can no way be happy in himself, or within his own compass, but sees all is to be had in and from the Lord Jesus; until then, he will not go out of himself, nor cleave to or follow the Lord Jesus Christ fully.

Now then, the other humiliation is defective in this, in that it cuts not a man wholly off from himself; the foundation is not laid low enough, there is wanting depth of earth; there is indeed so much earth as shall bring forth a green blade of profession, and such a foundation that there may be erected a slight building upon; but it is not low enough to bear a substantial building that shall stand out all winds and weathers.

This true humiliation hath these two things which go with it. 1. A man sees no foundation in himself. 2. He seeth a foundation out of himself to stand upon, and so he casts himself upon that, clasps about Christ, and wholly adhereth unto him, and so draws all sap and life from him, as the branch doth from the root, and thence comes that resolution and ability to cleave to the Lord, and to please him in all things. As the resolution to do it, so all his ability to go through with it; for being joined to Christ, there comes the Spirit of grace, called the virtue of Christ's death, because it works a virtue like unto his death into the heart: but, when the heart is not in this manner broken, many take up purposes and good desires, but are not able to keep them, because they were founded on their own strength; whereas, if the heart were broken from itself and engrafted into Christ, such purposes, made in his strength, would thrive and grow there. For if the soil be made good, and fit plants be planted in it, it is certain they will thrive. Now in a good heart those desires that are planted there thrive and wither no more; and though there may now and then waves arise, and they may be tossed to and fro, yet substantially they do not wither nor fall from the foundation. Those therefore who have begun a good course for a year or a month, and go not on in it, it is a sign they want humbling: he that is truly humbled falls back no more. Manasseh did not, nor St. Paul; "Lord, what wilt thou have me do?" said he then; and he was as good as his word. Therefore, you that have fallen away, take knowledge what the defect hath been, and wherein; for that will be a mean to set you right, and recover you again.

Another property of humiliation is, to have all the affections moderated, all delights in worldly things faint and remiss, and all the affections taken chiefly up about grace and sin: true affection will eat up the false. Such a person esteemeth spiritual things at a high rate, and all other things as little. Ask him what of all things he would desire, and he will tell you, Christ, and the favour of God, and the graces of the Spirit, and to have his lusts mortified and his sins pardoned; and that he is not anxious for the things of this life, he cares not in comparison whether he be poor or rich, bond or free; notwithstanding, if he may have a better condition he will use it rather. As a man that is condemned to die little regards his estate or the things of this life, his apprehensions are taken up with greater things; give him his pardon, and take all things else: so one truly humbled counts the favour of God so great, that he esteems all things else light in comparison. When, therefore, men are violent in their affections towards worldly things, and in their desires and delights in them, and endeavours after them, it is a sign that they are not humbled.

Another property is to love God and Christ much. Mary loved much, because much was forgiven her; that is, not simply that much was forgiven her, but because withal she had possession of it, apprehended it as much, and her sin great by a work of humiliation, and so she apprehended it a great matter to be pardoned. And so, a man having once apprehended death, and hell, and the wrath of God as belonging to him, when God comes on a sudden and tells him, Thou shalt live, when his neck was on the block, and he expected nothing but death, this causeth a man to love God much, and to prize Christ; and this made St. Paul also to love Christ so much, that "the love of Christ constrained him"—Because "I was a persecuter and a blasphemer," and he died for me, forgave me a great debt.

He that is truly humbled will be content with any condition, as the prodigal son; "I am no more worthy," says he, "to be called thy son; make me as one of thy hired servants." He was content to do the work of a servant, to live in the condition of a servant, to have the lowest place in all the family. So St. Paul looked on himself as the least of all the saints, and thought he could never lay himself low enough. Now this contentment is exercised about two things.

(1.) In a contentment in the want of outward good things. When a man is content with the meanest services and the least wages, to want wealth, and credit, and gifts, as Jacob when truly humbled, "I am not worthy of the least of all thy mercies;" whereas another man that is not humbled, when he looks upon himself, and God's mercies which he enjoys, he, thinking highly of himself, thinks himself too big for them, and that the disproportion is rather on his side; whereas Jacob, though he then had many mercies, yet said, Take the least mercy, and lay it in one scale, and myself in another, and I am too light for it, less than it, and it too much for me.

(2.) It is exercised in bearing crosses. One that is truly humbled still blesseth God, as Job, and bears and accepts the punishment of his iniquity willingly and cheerfully; as we see it made a condition, "If their uncircumcised hearts be humbled, and they bear, or accept of the punishment of their iniquity," Lev. xxvi. 41; if the Lord lay upon him a sharp disease, say the plague, loss of reputation, or poverty, yet he beareth it willingly and cheerfully; for, when a man thinks in earnest that he is worthy to be destroyed, whatsoever befalls him from God which is less than destruction, he blesseth God for it, and rejoiceth that he escapeth so.

The humble man, therefore, is in all conditions contented, always cheerful and blessing God: if he hath good things, they are more than he is worthy of; if evil, though ever so sharp, yet they are less than destruction, and less than he deserves; whereas an unbroken heart is always turbulent, and thinks in its secret murmurings that it is not well dealt with.

I should come now to the application of this doctrine; but I must resolve a case and scruple which troubles the hearts of many.

The case in question is—Whether to right and true humiliation it be necessary that such a solemn humiliation and such a measure of sorrow and violent legal contrition go before it.

I answer: There is a double kind of sorrow wrought in the hearts of men: the one is a violent tumultuous sorrow, which ariseth from the apprehension of hell and punishment, the ground whereof is self-love, and is commonly in those who are suddenly enlightened, and so amazed therewith being taken on the sudden; as we see in St. Paul, who was taken suddenly as he was going to Damascus; and it was discovered to him, that he was guilty of so great a sin, as he could never have imagined, till the voice from heaven struck his ears suddenly, "Why persecutest thou me?" And this we find by experience to have been in many who never have true humiliation, as we see in Judas.

God indeed sometimes useth it to bring men to true humiliation, as he did in St. Paul.

But again, we find in some a cleaving to God, and holiness of life, and a constant care to please him in all things, without this violent vexing sorrow. And many have had their hearts deeply wounded, amazed, affrighted, and have thereupon taken up great purposes which have come to nothing; the ground whereof having been merely a violent passion, the root withered, and so the fruit withered also: but a true apprehension and conviction of sin, as being in itself the greatest misery, is more real, and draws the heart nearer to Christ: so that in this case we may say of these two sorts, as Christ said of those who were bidden to go into the vineyard, "They that said they would go, did not, and others that said they would not go, yet went." Therefore we answer, that it is not always necessary to have such a violent sorrow, or that a man should lie any long time in such an evident sense of wrath; though always there is a right apprehension of sin which doth humble a man: which will appear by these considerations.

1. That is not always the greatest sorrow that is thus violent, though it seem to be so: it is not always the greatest sorrow which melteth into tears. As that is not the greatest joy that discovers itself in laughter, that is not the greatest sorrow which works the most violent commotion in the heart. There is a sad, silent, quiet sorrow that sinketh deeper, that wets more slowly, and soaks into the heart, and makes the heart more fruitful in the issue; which ariseth out of a more spiritual conviction of judgment, and of the evil of sin: though less passion accompanies it, yet a stronger and deeper affection of sorrow is wrought. I call it deeper, because it is more constant and

lasting, more to the purpose; the one being as a land-flood, the other as a spring.

2. Such a violent sorrow should be greater, yet it is not always alike necessary, neither on God's part nor man's.

Not on man's part: as some diseases do not need such sharp and quick a medicine as others, as some men's flesh is harder to heal than others, so some men's hearts have more stubbornness in them than others. Some have made themselves children of the devil by their wicked courses, worse than they were at first; others, in comparison, are but as the children of Adam, still as they were born, and therefore the same work may be wrought in them with much less ado.

On God's part it is not always so necessary, but is proportioned to God's ends; and God differs and is various in his ends concerning men. He intends to bestow a greater measure of grace upon one than upon another; and where he intends to set a greater building, there he digs a lower foundation. He purposes to use some as means to comfort others, and therefore letteth them see and feel more the bitterness of sin, that they may be "able to comfort others with the same comfort wherewith they have been comforted." He differs in the means to attain his ends: if he purposes to bring them to the same measure of grace, yet he will not go always the same way to work; as he often doth that without affliction, which sometimes he doth with it. As a man is brought to the same haven divers ways: some in a calm are tided in, others are driven in with a storm, but it is enough that they come in; so the promise is made to those that come to Christ.

3. A third consideration is, that it is not for want

of this greatness of humiliation that divers persons have not so violent a sorrow, but from some circumstance in the work itself; as,

(1.) Because the light of comfort comes in sooner to some than to others; they have the remedy presently after the wound is given. God, having broken the heart, bindeth it up again immediately. A man may have as deep a wound which a mitigated medicine, coming near to the bottom of the disease and soon applied, may sooner heal than another less deep, to which the remedy is not applied till a long time after, which therefore takes more time to cure. So also it is in joy, suddenness increaseth it for a while. For example, suppose a man is condemned for high treason, and brought to the block, and verily expects death, and his pardon suddenly comes, there is a great sensible change wrought in him, and therefore how excessively doth he rejoice! But take one who is guilty of the same fault, who knows that if he have not his pardon, he should lose his life, but hath his pardon directly after the sentence passed; he will prize his pardon, as much as the other, though he may not be so turbulently affected as the other.

(2.) It falls out thus by reason of the ignorance some have lived in before, who therefore are suddenly enlightened to know their estates; whereas another hath been brought up in knowledge, and the knowledge of his misery being let in by degrees, then the case doth also differ. As between two men who were to go through a wood, whereof one is set upon by thieves, not suspecting any, and is put into a fear of his life, and knows not how to escape, but one comes suddenly and rescues him and gives him his life: but the other is warned before, and knows he must go through such a passage, and that unless he hath a strong guard to go along with him, he will certainly perish. This man apprehends the danger as great as the other, and the benefit as great, and the love of him that should go with him as great; only his passion, either of fear or joy, is not so violent as the other's, though he truly rejoiceth in the deliverance as much as the other, and thinks himself as much bound to the man that delivered him.

I have spoken these things because some are scrupulous on the point, and think they may not safely apply the promises, because they have not had that measure of sorrow which others have had. But let no man suffer his assurance to be weakened for want of this, for a man may have as high an esteem of Christ, and be as thoroughly convinced of sin, though he want that violent work which God works in some, even a great sense of his wrath, and lets them lie there and then speaks peace; so that these are wrought by distinct acts and causes in a great distance one from the other, so that as their sorrow was evident, their joy was likewise evident. In another he works so, that as soon as the man sees sin, he also sees God pardoning.

And in those that have a violent shining of affection in their first humiliation, so much of it as is violent will vanish, but what is substantial will hold; so that even they in the end will come to this solid conviction of judgment at last, which only is constant and abideth with them. Therefore let not thy assurance be weakened for the want of this, for faith unites to Christ, and establisheth us in well doing.

But you will say, Is it not good to get that lively sense and view of sin?

I answer, Yes; for to that end God leads through crosses, and suffers thee to fall into sins, that thou mayest see the vanity of the creature and the sinfulness of thy nature; that when thou comest to heaven thou mayest say by thy own experience, It was not by my own righteousness that I came hither. Therefore, though it be good to get a sense of thy sin, yet let God go his own way, and use his own manner of working, whether by legal terror or otherwise. What he sees good for thee he will do to humble thee, but do thou use means to understand the law, thy own heart and actions, so that, when thou art fallen into new sins, thou mayest labour to see what a case thou wouldest be in if Christ had not delivered thee.

But let not thy assurance be weakened, for you must know there are but two main ends of humiliation, which if they be attained in thee, thou needest not call in question thy estate: (1.) It serves to make thee willing to match with Christ. We are Christ's spokesmen, and woo you every sabbath-day; but we find all the world like them who think themselves beautiful, and rich, and that they have matches enough; who though they are contented to have Christ for their Husband in heaven, yet not on the earth, with all those crosses they must take him with. Now humiliation comes and makes men willing; when a man comes to see and say, I have no such thing in me as I imagined, no riches, &c., but I am in debt, and shall be arrested and laid in prison, and my life must go for it, unless Christ will marry me; in that a man sees he shall be kept from all arrests by him; this makes a man willing to match with Christ; yea glad, though he have many crosses follow in this life upon the marriage. Now, therefore, if thou findest this wrought that thou canst sincerely say, I am willing to take Christ, and to be subject to him in all things, to follow him in all conditions, to give a full consent to take him, as I find that he in the word hath a full consent to take me; then certainly thou art humbled: not else. If thou hadst taken him only in a fit, and not out of judgment, thou wouldest have repented thee ere now. (2.) The second end which humiliation serves, is for sanctification, as the other helped him in his justification, that every unruly lust may be broken and mortified in him; that he might fear to offend, and be pliable to the Lord in every thing: whereas another, that is unbroken, quarrels with every thing, thinks his work too much, and his wages too little, and knows not why he should go a contrary way to the world. But an humbled man will do all this cheerfully, like a well-trained horse that turns at every check of the bridle, when another casts his rider. Dost thou find that thou tremblest at the word, and fearest sin, and darest not venture on it, and as for duties thou darest not neglect them, and this thou hast experience of in the whole course of thy life? then surely this work of humiliation hath been in thy heart: though thou seest not the fire, yet, if thou findest the heat, it hath been there; for these are the effects of it. And as I speak this for the comfort of those that have not felt such violent sorrows, so let me, on the contrary, say to others, who, it may be, have had such fits of sorrow, that if they find an unwillingness to submit thus to Christ, find their necks stiff to the Lord's yoke, and such an unbrokenness in them, that they cannot live without satisfying this or that lust, but can sin and bear it out well enough— that, let their sorrow have been ever so great, it is now past and gone, and was not right. Let men therefore examine themselves by the effects, for men are deceived on both sides.

The use is for exhortation, to stir up to the duty.

This exhortation I direct to two sorts of men; 1. To those who are already truly humbled, and, 2. To strangers to it.

1. You that are already humbled, and have obtained the assurance of the forgiveness of your sins, you must be humbled more; for, if the Lord grants gracious promises to the humble, this duty is to be done daily. When God requires us to be holy, (and his promises are made only to such,) there can be no excuse. There may be a hinderance in preparative humiliation; a man may be swallowed of too much sorrow: but not in this, which is a duty of sanctification. And know this, that all degrees of grace arise from the degrees of this true humiliation; which I make good to you thus: faith and love are the great radical graces, all the other graces are but branches springing out of them; now, they are strengthened by this humiliation: and graces, the more they grow, there is an addition still made to them, as there is an addition made to our humiliation.

(1.) For faith. Know that the more strongly a man lays hold on Christ and prizeth him, the more he goes on to apprehend his sin, and is emptied of himself; and though a man took Christ truly at his first conversion, yet there are degrees of prizing him. When a husband takes a wife, though at their first marriage there was such love between them as they would have chosen each other before any other in the world, yet their love may admit of degrees. After marriage they may see more grounds of loving each other more, so that, though the match is made, yet they may be more confirmed in their choice, which may be made more full and absolute: so towards Christ the will and affections may be wound up to a higher pitch, which is done by a further degree of humiliation.

What is faith, but a laying hold of Christ? Now, the emptier the hand is, the further hold it takes; and the more we are taken off ourselves, the further we shall cleave to Christ. A man in a river, that is likely to be drowned, and hath a rope cast to him, will be sure to catch as fast hold as he can; you need not to bid him do so. And to this end it is that christians are still taught more and more by the Spirit to see the vanity of the creature, and the vileness of their natures; and they are led through this wilderness to humble them, that so Christ may have the higher place in their hearts. Again, the greater the thirst is, the greater will a man's draught be; and the more you add to your humiliation, the more will your thirst be after Christ, and you will drink deeper of the fountain of life, and draw more sap from him.

(2.) It increaseth your love; for thereby we come to see ourselves more beholden to God, as having a greater debt forgiven us. What made Mary love much, but because she was sensible much was forgiven her! Therefore labour more and more to be humbled, especially as you fall into new sins, which the Lord oft lets his own people do, that they may be humbled more: and the more light a christian gets to discover his own vileness and the vanity of the creature, the stronger he will grow in grace, and the more established in well doing.

2. For those who are strangers to this grace of humiliation. That they may come to be humbled, let them observe these two rules: 1. Labour to see the greatness of sin. 2. Labour to see your own weakness and inability to help yourselves. Do not weigh sin by common opinion, but in a right balance. Do not deal with your souls as some deal with their bodies; when their beauty is decayed, they desire to hide it

from themselves by false glosses, and from others by painting; so do we for the most part with our sins; we desire to hide them from ourselves by putting false glosses upon them, and from others by feigned excuses. But deal impartially with yourselves herein, and labour to see sin in its full vileness: and that you may do so,

(1.) Pitch upon some one great sin, and take it into consideration. Christ, when he would humble Paul, tells him of his persecution; "Why persecutest thou me?" And St. Peter, when he would humble the Jews, tells them of their crucifying Christ, Acts ii. 23: so Christ, when he would humble the woman, he reminds her of her adultery, John iv. 18. And the method that God takes when he would humble us, it is good for us to take: for as when a man goes to rub a great stain out of a cloth, by the same labour he rubs out other stains that are less. My meaning is, not that you should let other sins alone, when I exhort you to single out one; but to consider all particulars else also, though ever so small; the multitude of them will help to humble thee, as well as the greatness. When a man sees he hath many debts, though but small, of sixpences and shillings, yet, being many, the total may arise to a great sum, and make a man see himself bankrupt. Therefore set your sins in order before you, give the due weight to every sin, but yet especially let great sins be in your eye. Now, some sins are greater in their own nature, as fornication, swearing, and drunkenness; others are made great by their circumstances, as that they were committed against knowledge, with deliberation, as Saul sparing the Amalekites, and sacrificing before Samuel came, wherein a commandment to the contrary was distinctly given. So God aggravated to

Adam his sin; "Hast thou eaten of the tree, whereof I commanded thee that thou shouldest not?" We are not to take sins by number only, but also by weight; as when they were committed contrary to many promises and purposes, so that hardness of heart followed upon it.

(2.) Withal, labour to make sins present, though long since committed; look on them as if they were newly done. For though our sins be great, yet if we apprehend and view them at a distance they move us not; which is the reason why men, in their health, are not more affected with the thought of death, which yet is one of the greatest evils, and so apprehended by us when we come to die: the reason is, because it is then conceived to be afar off, and so men are not moved with it. Thus is it in our apprehension of sins also: the distance makes them seem small; there is not a near conjunction and application of the object and the affection, they are not brought nigh, but men look upon sins long since past as small; whereas, in truth, sins long since committed are the same in themselves, and in the sight of God, as they were when first committed, and therefore should be the same to thee. So a man that hath committed a treason twenty years ago may be executed for it now: and therefore Joseph's brethren remembered their sin as fresh, though long before committed, as if they had then committed it; their affliction revived in their consciences, and made it as present: but we usually look on sins past as none of ours. Job saith that the Lord made him "possess the sins of his youth:" he possessed them, that is, looked on them as his own. What is the reason that to men in jeopardy, as in a storm at sea, and in the time of sickness, their sins then appear so terrible and fearful? they apprehend them as present. Now, that which God doth by affliction let us labour to get done by meditation, and by faith to look on them as present; make use of that optic glass which will bring them near to thee; labour to have a true judgment of their greatness, and that they are the same; for therein lies true humiliation, when the judgment is rightly convinced to esteem them the greatest evil, though it be not accompanied with so violent and turbulent a sorrow.

(3.) When you have made them thus present, do not quickly make an end, but let sorrow abide upon your hearts; or the work is not so soon done. You will get into some rock or other, unless you are continually persecuted and followed by the apprehension of your sins, till you come unto the city of refuge. But do as David did, he set his sin before him, Psa. li. 3; and as St. Paul, to whom that sin of persecution was ever fresh in his memory, and always in his mouth, "I a persecutor," &c. In this case learn something of the devil, who when he would bring a man to be swallowed up of sorrow, his manner is to keep a man's sins still before him, nor will he let a man be at rest; therefore they are called the buffetings of Satan, 2 Cor. xii. 7, because he comes often with blow after blow, to discourage and amaze a man: now learn from that practice of his, to stay and dwell upon the meditations of your sins, and often to present them to your souls. The green wood, perhaps, will not burn without much blowing. It is a frequent pressing of arguments that works on the affections; and so here keep the object near the faculty, and at last it will work. Look not on thy sins by fits; let there be no interruption by worldly joys or pleasures, no intervals: and this is St. James' counsel, "Be afflicted, and mourn, and weep: let your laughter be turned to mourning, and your joy to heaviness. Humble yourselves in the sight of the Lord," James iv. 9, 10; that is, if you will have your hearts humbled, abstain from lawful delights for the time, get alone. So he bids them set apart a day, that they might have no interruption; and if that will not do it, sanctify another, Joel ii. 15; let not one spark go out ere another be struck, otherwise you will be always beginning, and never come to be humbled.

If you would come to lay your sins to heart, and be affected with them, then be sure you be not kept off by those false reasonings and excuses, which hinder men from being humbled, and keep their sins from coming in upon them: as, for instance, when a man comes to consider of his sins, " Ah but," says he, " am I not in a good state already? and then my sins are pardoned: for I have good desires in me and a good meaning; I mean harm to no man;" and thus he is kept from seeing himself a child of wrath. But consider that thou mayest have all these good things in thee, and more than these, and yet be a child of wrath; these may be found in thee but not to thy advantage to escape damnation; for, though these be in thee, yet they have not that full effect they should, for they overcome not that evil which is in thee: for, notwithstanding all these good things, thou art still a sabbath profaner, a drunkard given to company. I might go over all other sins: but, in a word, if these overcome not sin, they are nothing; if they had been effectual in thee, they would have driven out the darkness. All the good things thou hast avail not to thy salvation, because they make thee not a good man; yea, all these good things, and the good fits thou hast had, will help forward thy condemnation. Because thou hast profaned the truth in thy heart, and hast not put fuel to these sparks, which God in mercy did put within thee; because thou didst suffer such talents as these to lie hid in a napkin, will he not say, Thou art an unprofitable servant?

Another thing that is to be added to the sight of your sins to humble you, is to know that misery and vanity which is in yourselves. We see by experience that men will grant that they are great sinners, but what is the reason that yet, notwithstanding, they stand out? They do not know their own misery and vanity; and, though men are told again and again of their misery, yet they are not stirred. But when death comes, then they are humbled; and why? because then they see what God is, and what they themselves are; death shows them the vanity of the creature. So that the way to be humbled is to know how unable a man is to be happy within his own compass. And to this end consider,

The greatness of God and his power, and the terrors of the Almighty, that he is the God in whose hands is thy life, and ways, and all: and consider, that unless thou seriously lay thy sins to heart, this God is thy enemy, and him with whom for ever thou hast to do.

Again; consider *what a weak creature thou art;* think with thyself—A sickness may come on my body, a cross may come on my estate, yea, an apprehension on my soul, that may suck up the marrow of my bones; and, above all, I have an immortal soul in a vessel of clay; and when this glass, this shell is broke, what will become of this poor soul of mine? This would bring a man to the prodigal's case. Belshazzar saw this, when he saw the handwriting upon the wall. Would it not have been wisdom in him to have seen and acknowledged it before? Thou art well now; thou dost not know what alterations may befall thee in the year, and thou hadst better leave a thousand businesses undone rather than this.

And yet further, all this will not do it, *except the Spirit of God come on thee;* for to humble a man is a mighty work. Though Elijah should preach to you, yea, all the sons of thunder should come, yet without the Spirit they would not be able to humble you. Yea, God himself came down from heaven upon mount Sinai, and with what terrors! and yet the people remained unhumbled, though they were amazed for a time. When Christ spake to St. Paul and struck him to the ground, if he had not a light within as well as without he had not been humbled: nor the jailor if there had not been an earthquake in his heart as well as in the earth. Jeroboam had as great a miracle wrought before him as St. Paul: you may well think the drying up of his hand amazed him, yet it did not make him give over his sin; and what was the reason? there was a miracle in both, but not the Spirit. And if miracles were wrought before you, from day to day, yet unless God sent his Spirit upon you, you would not be humbled. See the necessity of the Spirit's help in admonitions also. Amaziah was admonished by a prophet as well as David by Nathan, yet he was not humbled; and so we see some are humbled by afflictions, and others not. Therefore pray that God would send his Spirit to convince you; and learn also not to be offended at us, when in preaching the law your consciences are troubled. It is the Spirit that troubleth you, else our words would not trouble you; and therefore be not angry at us. And therefore also do not put off this duty of getting your hearts humbled; for thou art not able so much as to humble thyself: therefore take the opportunities of the Spirit, when he stirs thy heart.

But you will say, This rather discourageth us from the work; for then we must ever wait like mariners, till the tide and the gale come, and I may as well sit still; for I may go about it to no purpose, seeing the Lord must do it.

I answer thee, that if thou wouldest go about it, and shut up thyself in private a day, and after that another, in the end God would send his Spirit. When Christ bade his disciples go and row, though they rowed all night to little purpose, yet Christ came at last, and they were on the other side shortly. It may be that thou mayest be about it a month or two ere thou findest the Spirit coming; yet he will come in the end, and then the work will be thoroughly done: for there is a promise that Christ will "baptize with the Holy Ghost as with fire," not only his disciples, but those also who never had the Spirit: for it is not only for increase, but to begin grace. Yea, if God hath given thee a heart to pray, and to consider this promise, so that thou hast taken up a resolution to set thyself to the work and to wait, the Spirit is already in thine heart when thou hast so done; the work is begun, though thou thinkest not so. Never plead thou canst not do it without the Spirit; for I ask thee this question, Didst thou ever commit a sin in which thou couldest say, I did it against my will? was there ever any duty which thou hadst a mind to do, that thou couldest say, thou couldest not do it? Thy heart tells thee, No.

Therefore set about this duty, which is the main; which therefore we have pressed much, because it is as a nail driven into a wall, on which other graces hang. Humility and faith are the great things which the master builders were occupied about, and indeed the foundation, which therefore above all you must look to; and these our exhortations should be as forked arrows to stick in you, and not come out again, and not as other arrows that wound only.

We have done with the negative part—That such as do not humble themselves have no interest in the promises.

We come now to the affirmative part, which is for comfort—That if any man doth humble himself God will hear his prayer; his sins shall be forgiven.

The doctrine is this—THE LORD WILL BE MERCIFUL UNTO THE HUMBLE.

The Scripture is plentiful to prove it, " God giveth grace unto the humble," James iv. 6; sanctifying grace, and also saving knowledge; for he shows his secrets unto the humble, Psa. xxv. 14; yea, he dwelleth in such, Isa. lvii. 15; he hath an especial eye to such: those eyes that run through the whole earth fix themselves on the humble man for good. " All things hath my hand made," (yet them he regards not in comparison,) " but to him will I look that is of a contrite spirit," Isa. lxvi. 2. He promiseth also to fill them with good things, to give them preferment and honour, to exalt the humble and meek; yea, he regards it so, that when evil men have humbled themselves, they have not gone away without some mercy; as when Ahab humbled himself, 1 Kings xxi. 27—29, God promised he would not bring the evil in his days. But the best of God's children, when they have not humbled themselves, God hath withdrawn his favour from them; as he would not look on David till he had humbled himself. All the world cannot keep a humble man down; and all the props in the world cannot keep a proud man up.

The following are the reasons why God respecteth humble men:

1. A humble man giveth God all the glory; and "Him that honoureth me," saith God, "I will honour." Now, a humble man doth as Joab did. Joab would not take the victory to himself, but sent for David. So the apostles; "Know that Jesus hath made this man whole," Acts iii. 16. And it is the humble man's wisdom in all actions not to set himself up, but to say, No matter how I be regarded, so God be glorified; and God will honour such. Therefore Christ in his prayer makes this a ground of being glorified by God, "I have glorified thee on earth; now, O Father, glorify thou me," John xvii. 4, 5. And in some such proportion God will deal with his saints.

2. Humility keeps a man within his own compass; but pride lifts a man up above his proportion, it puts all out of joint and breeds disorder, and that bringeth destruction; and therefore humility was defined by some of the ancients to be that which, from the knowledge of God and ourselves, keeps us to our own level. That whereas a proud man lifts up himself above his measure; as a member in the body that swells takes up more room than it should, like bubbles in the water, which should be plain and smooth; but humility brings all into its place again, gives the Creator his due, and sets the creature where it should be; and therefore God loves it.

3. It makes a man sociable, and useful and profitable to others. A man would not have a stubborn horse, that will not go in the team with his fellows, nor such high trees as overshadow others, that will not suffer them to grow by them, and yet bring forth no fruit themselves. A man will not keep a cow or an

ox that is always pushing: and such an one is a proud man. It is only the humble man that will live profitably amongst his neighbours, and will not go beyond his own bounds.

4. A humble man hath such a frame of heart as the Lord delights in; for he is fearful to offend, always obedient, ready to do any service, and is content with any wages, loves much, and is abundant in thankfulness. He cleaves fast to the Lord, because he hath no merits of his own; and keepeth under his lusts, because he knows the bitterness of sin; he resigns up his heart to the Lord to follow him in all things. He is a man beloved of the Lord; so it is said of Daniel, when he had humbled himself, Dan. ix. 23; such an one as the Lord would have, and so it makes him fit for favour; and when a man is fit for favour, he shall be sure to have it, for God is not straitened toward us.

Use 1. Hath the Lord said it, and that from heaven, that if a man doth humble himself he will forgive him?—then this is a matter of great consolation: for now we can say from God to any one that droops, that if thou dost and wilt humble thyself, the Lord will forgive thee: consider it, this is news from heaven.

Put the case, (to compare spiritual things with things which you are more sensible of,) that thou hadst committed high treason against the king, and hadst forfeited thy life and goods; if any one should come from the king to thee, and tell thee that if thou wouldest go to him and humble thyself, it would be pardoned: and is not our case the same? We are guilty of eternal death, and have forfeited life and all; when therefore God himself says, If thou wilt humble thyself, thy sins shall be forgiven, what comfort is it! such a word as this should not be lost. A man that knows the bitterness of sin, would wait and wait again to obtain such a word as this from the Lord's mouth, and would keep it as his life. It was not a light thing to get such a word as this from God; none but a favourite could get it, nay none but his Son, and he only by his death: if Christ had not provided this charter for us, every man would have died in his sins. Now this we can and do say from God through Christ, that though your sins be great, and you have fallen into them many a time, and committed them with the worst of circumstances, yet if thou humblest thyself thou shalt be forgiven; so as thou mayest say, I may challenge God of his promise, and put this bond in suit, and he cannot deny it. This is a great matter; if a man will but seriously consider what it is to have this great God, the Governor of the world, to be an enemy, one would judge that he would think this gospel good news.

But you will say, I do yet neither know distinctly what it is to humble myself, neither can I humble myself; there is not a harder thing than it is. Therefore I will show it you once again, that you may know it; for why should we not in so great a point turn it every way, and mould it for your use, and to your apprehensions, as also that you may not think it harder than it is, by which the devil keeps many off?

Now, you may know what it is by the conduct and expressions of those who have humbled themselves. David having numbered the people, when he humbled himself, said, "Lord, I have sinned, and done very foolishly." Josiah's heart melted before the Lord. And Daniel was ashamed, "Lord, we have done wickedly, &c., and confusion belongs to us," Dan. ix. 5, 7. And Job, when he humbled himself, said, "Lord, I abhor myself, and repent in dust and ashes." And the prodigal, "I have sinned against heaven and before thee, and am no more worthy to be called thy son." And so they are said to be "weary and heavy laden." Many other expressions there are, but I will digest all into two heads. To humble a man's self is but to bring his heart and mind into these two acts.

(1.) Out of a sense of our unworthiness, to say thus unto the Lord: "O Lord, I have done exceedingly wickedly, and am worthy to be destroyed. I have been in the wrong way, and done exceeding foolishly; but thy ways are righteous, and thou art just: yea, I have dealt unthankfully and unequally with thee, who hast been so good to me." It was that which melted the heart of Josiah, and made Job abhor himself—"As vile as the dust I tread upon, as ashes that are good for nothing, or but as sackcloth, in which they used to humble themselves, the worst of garments, I am ashamed and confounded."

(2.) A sight of our worthiness to be destroyed, inability to help ourselves, and of the vanity of all things else. A man must further say, "I am not only unworthy, but guilty of death. My sins will break my back; I am not able to stand under them, and I am utterly undone: and when I look upon all the props of my life, my health, riches, &c., I see they are but vain things, reeds and feathers, and as hollow ground whereon I can set no footing: therefore, Lord, be thou a rock to me, on which I may rest and build myself." That this sight of our own inability is also necessary, we see by that scripture, "Charge them that are rich, that they be not high minded, nor trust in uncertain riches," 1 Tim. vi. 17: they are both joined together, for so far as a man doth trust in them, he is high minded; and the soul of man doth trust in them so long as it apprehends substance in them, and that they are not vanity; so far the heart bears itself upon them, and so is careless of the Lord. And why else do afflictions humble men, as Manasseh, but because a man then sees the emptiness of all things? They bring him to say with the prodigal, "I perish with hunger," and these cannot feed me; and bring him to hold fast to the Lord, which a man must needs do, when he hath but one thing to hold to. Now, when thou art wrought on so as to express this unfeignedly, this is to humble thyself.

Use 2. We should hence learn to strengthen our faith. If thou hast done this, if thou hast thus humbled thyself, confessed thy sins, taken up a full resolution to forsake them, thou shalt have mercy, according to that promise, "He that confesseth and forsaketh his sins shall have mercy," Prov. xxviii. 13.

But here we find those who have humbled themselves come in with two objections, that hinder their comfort. 1. That they cannot mourn for their sins. 2. That they fall into the same sins again and again, and that therefore they have not humbled themselves. Now, as we would not have the false deceived with false evidences, so neither would we have the true dejected, and therefore we will answer these objections.

If thou art so far convinced in thy judgment of thy sin and misery, and inability to help thyself, as that it hath turned the bent and rudder of thy will, so that thou sayest, I will go and humble myself to my Father, change my course, confess and forsake my sins; thou hast good evidence that thou art in a state of grace. For I ask, to what end is mourning and weeping required, but to awaken a man to come home to God in this manner? When, therefore, thou findest these effects, thou mayest be sure of thy safety. Suppose a man carries about him a deadly disease, so that upon the discovery and knowledge of it he is content to part with all that he hath to the physicians, and is cautious of meddling with any food that will hurt him and increase it; if he know that it is deadly, though he hath no sense of pain, (and there are some diseases, wherein a man feels not much pain, that yet are mortal,) it will make him as careful to use the means: and so it is here; if the conviction of the sinfulness and deadliness of sin work in thee those dispositions mentioned, then thou hast the end which mourning tends to.

Though thy affections be not so stirred, consider the promises are made to one's coming in, and taking Christ, and believing in him; they are not made to the commotion of the affections. And, in the words which we are illustrating, the promise is made to humility arising out of solidity of judgment. It is no matter by what means you are brought to take hold on Christ, so you come to him. It is all one whether I come to my journey's end by land or by water, on horseback or on foot, so I come thither.

If thou findest thou doest the things that an humble man should do, then, though thy affections seem not to be moved, yet in very deed they are moved and changed: as if thou art fearful to return to thy sins, and art resolved to please God in all things in thy power. For what are affections, but divers positions and situations of the will, and the feet it walks upon? they are but the divers motions and inclinations whereby the will shoots itself into the objects of it. Now look, which way thy will is resolved and set, that way are thy affections set also. If thou seest one rise up soon and go to bed late, to avoid poverty and to get riches, a wise man will assure himself that his aim is such, and his heart set upon riches; his actions show that his affections do move strongly that way, though he says he feels no such stirring. Therefore, though thou findest this stillness of affections, yet, if thou doest the same things that those do who mourn and weep more, thou mayest assure thyself thy affections are moved.

I add this, that it is no wound, if thy affections be not so sensibly stirred, if thy humiliation yet be found; for it is the nature of the affections to shoot into their own objects calmly, and to run along quietly, as water and wind doth; if they meet with no obstacle. The wind riseth if it meets with trees, and if the tide meet with the wind then the waves rise; so, if our affections be crossed, we are sure to hear of them then. If thou hadst not some hopeful assurance of thy estate, thou wouldest hear of mourning and drooping; it may be that the work of grace in thee hath always gone evenly on, the stream hath run calmly and quietly; but yet such do find that upon some sudden accidents or drawings nigh, when the Lord is pleased to make an impression upon them, then they hear of stirring affections.

But, to conclude all: know and resolve upon this, that the flowing and ebbing of thy affections is not that which thy salvation depends upon, but solidity of conviction of judgment which turns the will, and makes thee to cleave fast unto Christ.

Whereas you object that you fall into the same sins again and again; I answer, You may fall again and again, and into great sins, for which you have been soundly humbled. Why should we speak that which the Scripture doth not? only take it with this caution

—see that you are constantly warring against your sins, as Israel with the Amalekites, so as never to cease to look upon them but as your greatest enemies, and never be reconciled though you be foiled again and again. For what is true humiliation, but to reckon sin the greatest misery? for if a man reckon any greater, as loss of wealth, &c., then he would rather fall into sin than lose his wealth; whence it is that falseness of heart doth arise: but humiliation makes a man reckon sin such an evil, that he had rather suffer any thing than make a truce with sin. And the ordinary power of grace in a man's ordinary whole course is not seen in keeping men from relapses altogether, but in setting sin and the heart at odds, as health and sickness. Whilst a man is a living man he cannot be friends with any disease, for nature will resist it; it sets them at variance, as the spring and mud; and living waters will cleanse themselves, though the mud arise a thousand times. So, if thou reckonest sin the most destroying thing in the world, whence is this but because humiliation hath made that impression and apprehension of it on thy heart? This God hath set on thy heart as a brand in the flesh that will never wear out, and thou wilt fight against every sin and never be reconciled to it. If thou find this the constant disposition of thy mind, keep thy assurance strong, though many weaknesses be discovered in thee. It is utterly a fault among you to weaken your assurance by your daily slippings and failings, and Satan labours for that above all other, for then, when your assurance and hope are gone, you walk unevenly, and are as a ship that hath lost her anchor, or is without a rudder. Thou mayest sometimes feel a hardness in thee, and yet if this aforesaid be the constant disposition of thy mind, weaken not thy assurance, but say, Though I often find my heart hard and careless, froward and angry, whereas I should be meek and humble, yet I will not question the main, but I will go and renew my humiliation, which will strengthen my assurance. Hold this firm, for it draws into nearer communion with God and further from sin, establisheth a man in well-doing, and makes him abound in the work of the Lord.

Use 3. Learn hence also, that it is not enough for a man only to be patient in afflictions, but he must also humble himself under them. We must not only bear the cross, but willingly and cheerfully acknowledge God's justice in it, and our own sin; for to be humbled is a further thing than to be patient, as in 2 Chron. xii. 6. When the people were left in the hand of Shishak, it is said, that "the princes of Israel humbled themselves, and they said, The Lord is righteous;" where being humbled is expressed by acknowledging God to be righteous, which is more than to be patient. God looks for this in all afflictions, therefore he says, in 1 Pet. v. 6, " Humble yourselves," and not be patient only, " under the mighty hand of God, that he may exalt you in due time." Many a man in affliction may say that he will be patient; but that is not enough, he must humble himself, which is more than patience; for patience is only to bear it contentedly; but a man must go to God, and say, " Lord, I confess I am sinful, and have deserved more than this punishment; I wonder not at thy judgment, but at thy long-suffering rather, that it is no worse with me, the least of saints, and the greatest of sinners." So we see it was with Naomi, in Ruth i. 20, 21 ; " Call me not Naomi, [that is, pleasant,] but Marah, [that is, bitter ;] I went out full, and the Lord hath brought me home again empty; and the Almighty hath afflicted me;" and, seeing he hath afflicted me, I will carry mysel. accordingly. This is truly to humble a man's self. And thus did David, when he fled before Absalom; "Let the Lord do to me as seemeth good unto him," 2 Sam. xv. 26. And so said Eli, "In all this the Lord is good;" that is, The Lord is just in all this, and I and my sons deserve it, and more. Thus, when a man thinks it reasonable that God should punish him, he blesseth God that the cross is no greater, without complaining or repining. If the Lord leads thee through a variety of conditions, say with Paul, " I know how to be abased, and how to abound," and how to go through bad report as well as good report; and I am not only content, but cheerful in all this, and would be if it were far worse.

Use 4. If the Lord hath said that he will be merciful to the humble, then let us humble ourselves more and more, and get our hearts lower and lower, seeing there are such mighty and large promises belonging to the humble. And know, that as the Lord suspends his promises upon this, so they shall be fulfilled upon the performance of this; and, as we do this more or less, so shall the promises be fulfilled to us more or less; therefore let us do this more and more, for if we humble ourselves the Lord will fill our hearts with good things. When he sees a man taking a low place, he will say, Sit up higher. All the world cannot hold down a humble man, because the Lord setteth to his hand to raise him up; neither can it keep up a proud man, because the Lord setteth himself to depress and debase him. When the wall swells, it is not likely to stand long; when a joint is put out and swelled, it cannot be saved and set till the swelling abate. He hath "respect to the low estate of his handmaiden," so saith Mary, the blessed virgin, Luke i. 48. So God dealt with Naomi; he was long in humbling her, and then he raised her up. So with Job; when he was humbled, then God doubled his estate. Thus God deals with the humble, and that constantly; he never does any great things for any man till he hath first humbled him. How much was Joseph humbled before he fulfilled that promise to him that the sun, moon, and stars should bow to him! that is, his father, and mother, and brethren should obey him; and yet again, before God made good these promises to him, what ado there was to humble him further! which doubtless made him more to prize these mercies, and to be more thankful to God for them. So also in God's glorious appearances to Abraham, Isaac, and Jacob, he would still beforehand humble them, and make them low by some affliction or other before he would make any gracious promises to them. When Jacob was flying from the face of his brother, and was in great straits, and so made low in his own eyes, then did God first appear to him. When a man is humbled, it is the next door to preferment one way or other. Therefore it should be our wisdom to humble ourselves more and more, since there is so much benefit to be gotten by it. "By humility and the fear of the Lord are riches, honour, and life," Prov. xxii 4. The rule holds constant, the Lord makes it good; let a man be humble, and fear God, that is, allow himself in no sin, and the Lord will make it good one way or other, in his time.

But you will say, We see the contrary; proud men are advanced, and humble men depressed; they have riches, whereas the humble man is poor; and, as we used to say, where the hedge is lowest, there all the beasts go over, and tread the corn down: every man will be ready to trample upon the humble man.

(1.) I answer; The Lord gives outward, gaudy things to proud men, but he gives his jewels to those that are humble; he reveals his secret to them. These are princes though they go on foot, and the others are servants, though they ride on horseback.

(2.) But even as it respects the things of this life, the Lord doth exalt the humble, and bring down the proud; only with this caution, he doth both in season, when things are brought to maturity: as the apostle Peter saith, " Humble yourselves under the mighty hand of God, that he may exalt you in due time," 1 Pet. v. 6. God doth it not on a sudden. When the proud, like the corn, are ripe, then he puts in the sickle, and cuts them down, and casts them into the fire. The wall which is swelled, must have a time to moulder and fall; and so, on the contrary, there is a due time for the exaltation of the humble. And therefore if thou sayest, I have humbled myself, and have not been healed, I have not been freed from such a temptation for all my humiliation; if this be thy case, then assure thyself thou art not humbled enough; but go thou and yet bring thy heart lower, and then be confident that this rule will hold. The Lord will take off the smarting plaster as soon as it hath eaten out the proud flesh: so soon as thy heart is truly humbled, the Lord will help thee; he will either remove the cross, or give thee that which is equivalent: and thus the Lord hath always done. So he dealt with Joseph. You perhaps may think, and he might have thought, that it was long before he was exalted; but yet that time was not too long, for as soon as the Lord had truly humbled him, then he immediately exalted him; as you may see in Psalm cv. 18—20, " Whose feet they hurt with fetters: he was laid in iron: until the time that his word came: the word of the Lord tried him. The king sent and loosed him." And so the Lord dealt with Job. All the time that his friends were reasoning with him, his heart would not be brought down; but, when the Lord himself came and reasoned with him, then he began to abhor himself in dust and ashes: and how soon after was he restored, and all he lost restored double! This being, as you see, God's constant course, if thou humble thyself and yet liest long under a calamity, thou mayest assure thyself there is something wanting in thy heart, and, therefore, be content with God's dealing. Lest St. Paul should be exalted, there was given him a thorn in the flesh, 2 Cor. xii. 7: if St. Paul needed humility, who doth not? Remember this rule, that if God's people humble themselves, then he will certainly help them; only it will be in due season.

But you will say, How shall we get down our stubborn hearts; pride is very natural, and the hardest thing in the world to overcome?

Let every man consider, whether he be released or not from the plague of his heart; if that hangs continually on thee, then know thou art not humbled enough. The meaning is, not that thou shouldest be brought to an apprehension and fear of hell; but thy heart is to be brought down more. Thou mayest be humbled truly, so as to be within the covenant, and yet not enough to have thy heart wrought to this or that frame God would bring it unto.

To bring your hearts lower, use these means:

[1.] Consider your hearts often. Consider what unruly lusts you find hid there; make it your daily custom to search into this. We go not a day's journey in this life, but there is somewhat discovered in our hearts which may serve to humble us further, as it was with them in the wilderness; "Thou shalt remember all the way which the Lord thy God led thee these forty years in the wilderness, to humble thee, to prove thee, and to know what was in thy heart," Deut. viii. 2. There is not one day but a godly-wise man may discern something in his heart, which may be matter of humiliation to him, which he saw not before; vainglorious speeches, unlawful silence, cowardice in good causes, worldly-mindedness, unruly affections, that will be still stirring; and something will be discovered without, in his actions also, which when he sees such sparks ascending, he ought to remember to look to the fire, the furnace within; these are but the buds, there is a deep root of bitterness within; consider these are but ebullitions, there is a spring within; search into all the corners of the house for this sour leaven. So the first means is studying ourselves, for the way to humble a man's self is to know himself.

[2.] And as you must study yourselves, so you must also study the Scriptures; that is, you must consider the strictness and holiness that is required of you therein, and lay that and your hearts together; apply this level and square to your ways, and it will discover the crookedness of them; dress yourselves by this looking-glass every morning, for it will show you the smallest spots; and this will exceedingly humble us. For this is a sure rule, degrees of humiliation follow degrees of illumination; as the more any man is enlightened, the more he is humbled. Hence he that is most conversant in Scripture, is most humbled.

[3.] And you must not only look to increase your light, but look to your hearts and ways, to keep yourselves upright, and to be constant in a holy course, and all holy duties; and this will help to increase your humiliation. Many abstain from holy courses and duties, because, say they, we are not humbled enough. It is indeed true we must begin with humility, yet this you must know, that the setting yourselves to a holy course is of itself a notable means to increase humiliation; for thy watchfulness will increase tenderness, and tenderness will increase thy humiliation. The hearts of men that are bold in sinning grow hard; and so, on the contrary, when men are fearful to offend their hearts grow tender.

[4.] But yet add to this, diligence in your callings; for, as the wise man saith, "The sluggard is more wise in his own conceit, than ten men that can give a reason;" that is, he is self-conceited and proud. A sluggard that hath nothing to do looks abroad to other men's matters, and looks not to his own ways, nor his own heart, which would be a means to humble him: therefore diligence is a great means to humble and bring down our hearts, because idleness is a means to lift them up.

[5.] And further: it is profitable for you to remember times and sins that are past. A man will be ready to say, "I hope I am changed now, what I have been I care not for;" but the Lord to humble David told him what he had been, "I took thee from the sheep-fold." So with the jews, "Thy father was an Amorite, and thy mother an Hittite," and "I saw thee in thy blood."

[6.] Be careful to distinguish wisely between thyself, and grace in thee; and that will be a means to humble thee. As Paul, in 2 Cor. xv. 10, "Not I, but the grace of God which was with me." If the Lord hath beautified us with many graces and gifts above others, we must not exalt ourselves above others; we must look upon ourselves, as considered in ourselves, to be the same men still. Can the wall say it hath brought forth the beams that the sun hath cast upon it? So if God hath shined upon thee, and left others in darkness, art thou the better of thyself? Shall the pen boast itself, because it hath written a fair epistle? Who made it? who put ink into it? who guided it? The glory belongs not to the pen, but to the writer. What though God hath used thee, and not others, in some great work? the praise is his, not thine: we praise not the trumpet, but him that sounds it. Paul was a better trumpet than ten thousand others, and yet he saith, "I am nothing." The smoke, a dusky and obscure vapour, climbs up into the light, rising above the pure air around it. Many exalt themselves above their brethren for gifts and outward things, which are but the trappings, and make not the difference between man and man; as if a man were the taller because he stood on a hill, or a man had a better body because he had a better suit on: he is the same man still. We are not to be proud, even of our graces, much less of outward things.

Use 5. Is the Lord thus merciful to the humble? then take heed of applying those promises to thyself without a cause when thou art not humbled.

But thou wilt say, I am humbled. It is well if it be so: but consider, hath thy humiliation brought thee home? Perhaps it hath brought thee out of Egypt; but hath it brought thee into Canaan? hath it driven thee to the city of refuge? to the horns of the altar? to thy Father's house? Many came out of

Egypt that never came into Canaan, but died in the wilderness. Art thou watchful over all thy ways, fearful to offend, looking to every step where thou settest thy foot, how thou hearest, how thou prayest, how every work is done, every word spoken, every hour spent? For this is certain, if he be humbled, it will dry up the fountain of sin, and make him wary in all his ways, and fearful to sin. Thus much for this first condition.

Sec. III. ON SEEKING GOD'S FACE.

2 Chron. vii. 14.

IF MY PEOPLE, WHICH ARE CALLED BY MY NAME, SHALL HUMBLE THEMSELVES, AND SEEK MY FACE.

We are now come to the next condition—"If my people seek my face:" where we may observe this point,

That, except a man seek God's face, all his labour in his humiliation and prayers, and whatsoever else he doth, is lost.

This is put in among those other conditions; and therefore without this the promise is not made to us. For the unfolding of this point we must first inquire what it is to seek God's face. It is to seek the Lord himself. Many, when they are in distress, will seek to the Lord for deliverance; in time of famine, they will seek to him for corn, and wine, and oil; but they seek not the Lord himself, nor communion and reconciliation with him; they seek to the Lord, but not the Lord: they seek what he can do for them, but not his person, not himself. "They have not cried unto me," says God, "when they howled upon their beds: they assemble themselves for corn and wine, and they rebel against me," Hos. vii. 14. They then wanted corn and wine, and sought them at God's hands; but not the Lord whom they had lost.

Thou mayest seek salvation and deliverance from

hell, out of the strength of natural wisdom, because it is for thy good; and also be convinced of the necessity of faith and repentance to escape hell and obtain salvation; and mayest thereupon go far in the performance of many duties, and be constant a while in them, and yet not seek the Lord's face in all these; therefore the Lord regards them not. A thief that is arraigned at the bar will cry earnestly for his life, but yet he seeketh not the face of the judge; that is, he doth it without love to the judge, only from the love of life: so we may do much to escape hell, and to attain the life opposite to it, and yet all this while not seek the presence of God, and then God regards it not. You find this disposition in yourselves, and see it in others: if a man be ever so observant of any of you, and perform ever so many offices of friendship to you, yet, if he loves you not for all this, you know that he doth not prize you, nor desire your love and favour so much for itself, but only for his own ends; in this case you care not for what he doth: so the Lord knows the heart and the reins, and what thine end is, whether it be communion with his person immediately, or thine own welfare merely; and if the latter, he regards not thy humbling thyself, nor thy prayers. The promise, you see, is suspended upon it: it is a distinguishing point, and will separate between the precious and the vile; it is a mark set upon God's people alone, to seek God's face, Psa. xxiv. 6.

We will therefore further and more particularly consider, what it is to seek God's face, or presence. And there are three ways to find it out.

I. By what is here joined with it; "If they humble themselves, and seek my face." By considering the connexion that these two have together, we may find out what seeking of God's face is. Now, there is a twofold humiliation wrought in men:

1. The one is, for that bitterness and punishment that sin brings with it; and this never brings forth either faithful prayers or seeking God's face.

2. But there is another kind of humiliation, which hath a further ingredient in it, and that is, the sight of the foulness of sin. Then God openeth a crevice of light to look upon sin, not only as that which brings bitterness with it, but as that which in itself is most filthy and abominable, and by that light it is made such in his account: for it is one thing to flee from the sting of the serpent, another thing to hate the serpent itself; and so, to take heed of the wolf because of his cruelty, and to hate the wolf itself, are different things. Other creatures may hate the properties and conditions of a wolf; but a lamb hates the wolf itself. Now, with this latter kind of humiliation there is an enlightening, whereby God shows to a man his own glorious face, the lustre whereof helps him further to see the foulness of sin. God, by the same light of the Spirit whereby he shows a man the ugliness of sin, discovers withal his own excellences, which makes the sinner, thus humbled, to seek his face, to seek grace as well as mercy. But other men either see not God's face at all, or only see his angry countenance; only those whom the Lord effectually calleth see his gracious face. Now, he to whom it is hid seeks not God's face; for none can seek it unless they have seen it; and he who sees it only as angry, flees from God: but he discovers himself to the truly humble; the secret of the Lord is with such, Psa. xxv. 14; and so Christ says, "I call you not servants, for the servant knoweth not what his Lord doeth: but I have called you friends; for all things

that I have heard of my Father I have made known unto you," John xv. 15. He reveals himself to those who are already his friends, or to those he is about to make his friends; one of the first things he doth is to reveal his face to them. With men, indeed, the custom is, first to be made friends, and then secrets are revealed; but contrarily with God: he reveals his secrets and his face to us, that we may be made friends with him, and then we grow into further acquaintance with him. They are therefore called the secrets of the Lord, because only revealed to the saints. Servants, indeed, see what is done in the house, but there are many things which their masters reveal not to them; and so many come to the house of God, and hear what is spoken of God and Christ, but yet there are certain secrets that are hid from them, told only to the children, the sons and daughters of God. The others hear as much and see as much of the outside as God's children do, yet the secrets of things are hid from them; and, among others, God's face and the excellences thereof are hid from him. This he reveals, as his other secrets, only to those that fear him; and this revealing is a special work of the Spirit. If a man would see the sun, all the stars in heaven and torches on the earth could not help him to see it; unless the sun itself ariseth and shines, and there come a light from the sun itself, you cannot see it; and so all the angels of heaven and all the wisdom of men on earth cannot show you God's face unless he opens the clouds and reveals himself by his own Spirit, it will not be done. He is therefore called the Spirit of revelation, Eph. i. 17, by which God reveals his secrets to his children; when he begins to call them effectually, they see him, and none else.

Preachers make known the doctrines about God and Christ to all alike, but the Lord makes the difference by revealing himself to one and not unto another; that which is said especially of the Jews, 2 Cor. iii. 15, 16, is in like manner applicable to us all. The Lord's face shines, as the face of Moses did, ver. 13, and he gives the knowledge of his glory in the face of Jesus Christ, 2 Cor. iv. 6, in the ministry of the word every day: but a vail lies upon all men's hearts, upon all but those whom the Lord calls, and upon theirs also till he calleth them, as upon the jews' hearts; "Nevertheless, when it shall turn to the Lord the vail shall be taken away," ver. 16: and until then God's face cannot be seen, as the face of Moses was not: and who shall take away that vail? The Spirit of the Lord. "Where the Spirit of the Lord is, there is liberty," ver. 17; and when he doth free us of that vail, then, "with open face, we behold as in a glass the glory of the Lord," ver. 18; that is, we see the amiableness of his face, the happiness of communion with him. When the light breaks through the clouds thus, and the Lord gives a glimpse of himself, then men see him, and never give over seeking his face more and more, till they have found him. If the other sort I spake of see him, they see only an angry face, and that makes men fly from the Lord. We see that in distress and at death many will do anything rather than go to God; they tremble at his presence, and no way desire it, as Adam did not, but flee from it: and thus would all do if no word were revealed. Therefore, the Spirit of revelation takes away the vail, and breaks the clouds, that his own elect may have a glimpse of his face; and the Spirit of adoption, who is sent down into their hearts, shows God as merciful, full of kindness and love.

They see not only his face, but his face shining in all gracious willingness to receive them. The Spirit presenteth him as a loving Father ready to admit them, and graciously to forgive and receive them. They see God's face, that is, both his excellency and beauty, and also his love and graciousness towards them; and this makes them seek his presence and reconciliation with him, and never to be at rest without it: like Moses, when he said, "Lord, if thy presence go not with me, carry us not up hence," Exod. xxxiii. 15. They desire nothing, can be content with nothing, but the presence of God, and communion with him; the light of his countenance.

II. The second thing whereby I express what it is to seek God's face, is to seek the Lord alone; without respect to punishments and rewards; in his own person, as considered in himself, in his attributes, in his holiness and purity; so as not to seek the things he brings with him, but to seek himself, and the things which are in him.

But you will say, This is very difficult, to set aside all respect to rewards and punishments.

I answer, it is an error to think that you may not make use of rewards and punishments: for,

1. Punishments and the threatenings of the Lord are the true objects of fear; and a faculty and a habit may lawfully be exercised about their proper object: thus rewards are the subject of desire, and so may lawfully be sought after and desired.

2. The Lord himself, in Scripture, useth these motives, of judgments on the one side, and of rewards on the other, and therefore we may make use of them to our own hearts; for to that end hath God propounded them.

Therefore I will set down two conclusions to clear

to you what use there may be made of rewards and threatenings.

1. The propounding of, and the respect unto, rewards and punishments, is a good beginning to draw us on to seek the Lord's face; it is a good introduction. The fear of hell may cause a man that hath not as yet seen God's face to reflect on his own heart and ways, and to be sensible of the evil of them; and so also the happiness of heaven may draw him on: but all this while he is but beginning. A woman considering with herself whether she should marry such a husband or not, beginneth to consider what she shall be without him, and what she shall have with him. She considers him perhaps as one that will pay all her debts, and make her honourable; and yet it may be she considers not the man all this while; and yet these considerations are good preparatives to draw her on to give entertainment to him; but, after converse and acquaintance with the person, she likes the person himself so well, that she is content to have him, though she should have nothing with him; and so she gives her full and free consent to him, and the match comes to be made up between them, out of true and sincere free love and liking. So it is here; men begin at first to consider their own misery most, and that if they should apply to other things as remedies their labour would be in vain, for there is a vanity in all things; and they cannot help themselves in trouble: therefore they judge they must go to the mighty God, who is able to do more than all to rid them out of misery: and they consider that, going to him, they shall have heaven besides. Now, all this may exist while they consider not the Lord's person; yet this consideration makes way, that God and we may meet and speak together. It brings our hearts to give way,

that the Lord may come to us; it causeth us to attend to him, to look upon him, to converse with him, to admit him as a suitor, and to be acquainted with him; and, whilst we are thus conversing with him, God reveals himself; and then, being come to the knowledge of him in himself by that his special light spoken of before, we love him for himself; then we are willing to seek his presence, to seek him for our husband, though all other things were removed from him. And now the match is made, and not till now; and then we so look upon him, that if all those other advantages were taken away, we should yet still love him, and not leave him for all the world; so that if we should imagine he would give us ever so much, and yet withdraw his face, we could not be at rest. Before, if a man could but be assured he should not go to hell, and should have creatures and comforts about him, it would be enough to him; but now it is not so. If God's countenance be now but clouded, if any breach be between him and God, he cannot rest till it be healed, and he see his face again.

2. Yet still, after the match is made, there is a second use of punishments and rewards; they are useful, not only to bring us in, but to confirm us also in our choice; they serve both as an introduction, and as a help, when we are come in, to confirm us in our choice: as when a woman is married, she, having this, has also many conveniences in addition. So it is with us, although the Lord alone be sufficient reward, so that if we had nothing else we should never repent of our choice, yet we having many good things with him, it helpeth us in our love to him, and confirms us in our choice. These are then good additions, but not good principles and foundations; and encourage us much if added, and put to seeking the Lord

for himself, as the principal. As ciphers added to figures help to make the number greater, though, if they stand alone, they are nothing; so these: and though they be not good leaders, yet they are good followers: they are as a good wind, that fills the sails, and sets the ship forward with the greater speed, when the rudder is once set right, to steer to God alone.

III. The third thing whereby I explain what is meant by seeking God's face, is to seek the Lord's presence in opposition to a man's self, with denial of himself; not serving his own ends in seeking the Lord, but giving up himself to the Lord alone. In all things an unregenerate man doth not know the Lord, is not acquainted with him, and therefore will not prefer the Lord to himself: but a regenerate man, that knows him, reckoneth all things, as life, liberty, riches, &c. but as dross, so that he may enjoy the Lord. He hath set up in his heart the Lord for his God, and desires not to stand upon his own foundation: and therefore when the Lord comes into competition with himself, and the matter is between God and his credit, &c. he is willing to deny himself.

But here the great objection is, how it is possible for a man not to seek his own happiness, safety, and advantage. This troubles many, and makes them think their sincerity but hypocrisy, and may put a scruple into the best: I will therefore clear this for their sakes whose hearts are upright, as also to exclude those whose hearts are not sound.

The answer stands upon these two points.

1. It is true that a man may seek and love himself, and desire his own happiness, yea, and all his actions may take their rise from thence, so as to be moved in seeking the Lord, in doing what he doth

with a respect to his own good and safety; and that this is so, take these reasons.

(1.) Because God hath commanded it, for he bids us love our neighbour as ourselves: where it is taken for granted that we must love ourselves, because loving ourselves is made the rule of loving our neighbour. Now to love a man's self, what is it but to seek a man's own good?

(2.) A man is commanded not to kill himself, or to hurt himself; and, by the rule of contraries, he is thereby commanded to seek the preservation of himself and his own good: for when we expound the commandment, "Thou shalt not kill," as referring to a neighbour, we say it includes this affirmative command, Thou shalt seek the good of thy neighbour: so, when we expound it of ourselves, we are to understand it as not only forbidding us to destroy ourselves, but as commanding to preserve ourselves, and to seek our own safety.

(3.) It is impossible for the creature not to wish its own happiness. The Lord doth not command that which is simply impossible even to pure nature; for it is the nature of everything that hath an appetite to desire that which is good for itself.

(4.) Self-love is a plant of God's own planting and therefore not to be rooted up. God did put it into us all, for it is the nature of everything to do so; and the work of nature is the work of the Author of nature.

(5.) Many motives which the Scripture uses are taken from self-love; as that of Christ, "Fear him that can cast both body and soul into hell:" and so when it promiseth us a kingdom. The Scripture deals with men by working upon this principle; and by arguments taken from ourselves. This is the means which the Holy Ghost employs, and leads a man into the ways of peace by, and we must not reject these means.

2. The second part of the answer is, that yet, notwithstanding, we may and ought to seek the Lord in opposition to ourselves; that is, when God and we come into competition, the commandment comes in opposition to ourselves; the case being such as that if we obey God we hurt ourselves; then we must prefer God and his commandments to ourselves.

But you will ask, How can this stand with the former; that a man should make his own good the source of his actions, and yet in his actions oppose himself? I answer, when once a man is persuaded that even to destroy himself is the best way to provide for himself, and that to let himself go, and his credit and life, and give up all to God, is that whereby he shall put himself into a better condition,—when a man is persuaded of this, then you see both do stand together. As for example, when Abraham would have destroyed his son by offering him up, he thought he should not lose by it, nor Isaac neither: he thought within himself, "God hath commanded me to do it, and I never yet lost by keeping any commandment he gave me. God is able to raise him up again. I never yet was a loser by him; but, on the contrary, I shall be sure to be a loser, and my son also, if I do it not." It is indeed impossible that if a man would simply be a loser that he would do thus; but he considers that though he be destroyed at present, yet he believes it will be for his good; and so it will be indeed. As, take a beam of the sun: the way to preserve it is not to keep it by itself; the being of it depends upon the sun: take the sun away, and it perisheth for ever. But yet, though it should be obscured, and so cut off for a while, yet, because the sun remains still, therefore when the sun shines forth again it will be renewed again. Such a thing is the creature compared with God. If you would preserve the creature in itself, it is impossible for it to stand; like a glass without a bottom, it must fall and break. When therefore this is considered by a man, then he will say, I am content to deny myself, and seek the Lord, when self comes into competition with any commandment of his.

And let not this seem strange to you, that the best way to make ourselves happy is to resign up ourselves to the utmost to glorify God. You see in common experience, that a corn which is fallen into the ground, if it continue whole, it perisheth; but, if it die, it brings forth a hundred fold; "That which thou sowest," says the apostle, "is not quickened, except it die," 1 Cor. xv. 36. The apostle there speaks of the resurrection: but we may truly apply it to the resurrection of a sinner here; that except a man die, that is, be willing to let all he hath go, and to expose himself to what the Lord shall put upon him, that he perisheth indeed; but if he die, then he is quickened; even in this life he shall have a hundred fold. And when this is thoroughly considered by a man, he will easily seek God's face in preference to himself. And thus, whenever a man suffers anything for a good conscience in obedience to God, it is the best way to provide for himself. That this is not a mere notion, will appear by comparing these places together: " Thou shalt love thy neighbour as thyself," and thou shalt love God above all, even above thyself, Matt. xxii. 37—39:

and with it also that other, "Thou shalt keep the commandments of the Lord, which I command thee, for thy good," Deut. x. 13. Now put both together: this is God's commandment, to love God above thyself; and all the commandments are given for thy good, therefore this amongst the rest. Denying ourselves, therefore, when God comes into competition with ourselves, is the best way to provide for ourselves: therefore set it down for a conclusion, that to have God alone, and thus to seek his face, is your happiness. The end of every thing is the perfection of it; now God is the end of the creature, and therefore to get him is to get thy perfection and happiness. Again, we have all from him, as the branch hath all from the root; and therefore the way for the branch to keep life in itself is to keep close to the root, and when it is broken off it dies: so we, so long as we cleave to, and seek the Lord, are preserved. And this was the ground which all the saints went upon in their sufferings, both of persecution and death. This was the case of Moses and Paul, when the one spake of being himself blotted out of the book of life, and the other of being accursed from Christ: that is, saith St. Paul, If this be for God's glory, and the good of his church, let me perish. In which, though they seem to imply immediate injury to themselves, yet they knew what was ultimately best for themselves.

And this is all the difference between a carnal man and one to whom God hath revealed himself: they both agree in this, they both love themselves, and seek their own happiness; but they differ in this, that they seek it in a different way; the one in the Lord, but a carnal man seeks it in himself and the creatures A godly man is so influenced by God, that he seeks him, and cares not what he loses to gain him; but another man, when he is told of an invisible God, will not trust to things unseen; the things he sees he will rest upon, and so seeks for a happiness within his own compass; and therefore, when self comes in competition with the Lord, he lets the Lord go.

But then another question requires to be answered, how these two should likewise stand together: to seek the preservation of a man's self, and yet to expose himself to injury, as Moses and St. Paul did. For answer, you must know that in every regenerate man there are two selves: the common nature, which is in every man, to love a man's self; and the spiritual, which leads to God. By the first, a man seeks himself immediately, and in the first place; by the other, he is carried to seek the Lord: and these two are reckoned two several selves in Scripture, and so expressed to us. First, flesh and corruption are called a man's self; "We preach not ourselves, but Christ," 2 Cor. iv. 5; that is, not for our own glory, which he calls himself, because men use to reckon it as themselves. So, "I knew a man in Christ,—caught up into paradise,—of such an one will I glory; yet of myself I will not glory," 2 Cor. xii. 2—5. By self he means the corruption which was in him, but there was something else in him, which he reckons as another man from this self. "A man in Christ;" of such a man I will rejoice, that is, of my regenerate part, which is a new creature in Christ; but not of myself, that is, of my flesh and corruptions, I will not rejoice, nor of the regenerate self, as of itself, but as it is in Christ, which is another expression. This corruption is called a man's self, because it is spread over the whole man, as the form through the whole matter; and a man will not part with it, but fights against every thing, fights against it as if it were himself.

And again, that the other regenerate part is called a man's self, which a godly man reckons so, rather than the other, we have Scripture authority for; "It is no more I, but sin that dwelleth in me," Rom. vii. 17; that is, not the regenerate part which I account myself, but sin which I account but an inmate, dwelling under my roof; which yet is called a man's self, for the reason already alleged, because spread over the whole man. It is now easy to conceive, how the preservation of himself may agree with exposing himself to destruction, and how a man may seek the Lord in opposition to himself.

In that which the flesh desires a man is bound not to seek himself, that is, not that self; but yet he may seek the good of his other self, and seek the Lord too, for God's will and it are in unison: and he may be said to seek God's face alone, though he seeks the desire of that self; for there is no difference, no opposition between them. And likewise that regenerate self may seek God in opposition to that other self, that is, what it desires, when it desires amiss, (for all those desires which are amiss are from that fleshly self,) and so we must not desire what we ourselves would desire, but destroy it, and the desires of it, and seek the Lord in opposition to it, which tends to the preservation of our regenerate self, and proves so in the end.

And that all this ought to be done, we will give you one reason, and so come to the uses. And that reason is drawn from the holiness of the Lord. "One angel cried to another, and said, Holy, holy, holy, is the Lord of hosts; the whole earth is full of his glory," Isa. vi. 3: this thrice holy cry was the proclamation of angels, and that upon this occasion. The Lord sends Isaiah the prophet to pronounce a judgment on his people, and that a great one, their rejection, and at the same time the angels are sent to proclaim God's holiness. Now, holiness is the appropriation of a thing to the Lord's use, and a sequestration of it from common use: and so the holiness of God himself, which is the rule of all other holiness, is an appropriation of his actions to himself, as his end. He is then said to be holy when he doth things for himself; therefore being about to do so great a work peculiarly for himself and his glory, as when he would destroy his own people, and destroy kingdoms for his own best advantage and ends, the glory of himself, then he lets them know this as the only reason, because he is holy; for if he should not respect himself, he would not be holy. So Rom. xi. 33—36. The apostle, having spoken of this rejection here prophesied, concludes with this, "How unsearchable are his judgments, and his ways past finding out! For of him, and through him, and to him, are all things: to whom be glory for ever." As if he had said, "God hath done all this, but I know not the reason of it, nor any one else; only God is for himself; for he being of no cause but himself, therefore he may do all for himself: if he were of another, he might do all for another, yea, otherwise he were not holy." Now if this be God's holiness, then the holiness of man is to do all for God; which he is therefore to do, because he is of another cause above himself, and therefore is to seek another end above himself, namely, the Lord; and then he is said to be holy, when he hath no eye to himself, but to God; when in his recreations, the use of riches, and in his whole course he hath this eye and aim at God, and not at himself.

The nature of holiness is expressed in two things 1. Purity: 2. Sequestration to God; so that holiness and chastity are much alike. Chastity in a wife consists in keeping close to her husband, and keeping herself apart from all others; and God's holiness consists in the purity of his nature, and in a sequestration of all things to himself. Now, our holiness is not so, but we, being of another cause, must do all for another end; our holiness consists therefore in giving up ourselves to the Lord: therefore, Isaiah says, " Sanctify the Lord, and let him be your dread;" as if he had said, "If you make anything else your dread, you do not sanctify the Lord." What he says of fear, is true of all other affections and actions; holiness dedicates all unto the Lord. Some actions are holy for the substance of them, as prayer, keeping the Lord's day, and all such immediate duties of his worship; some by putting a right end upon them: and so all actions may be holy, of what kind soever, as recreations, which are common actions, and eating and drinking, all which, when done to the Lord, become holy. It is the nature of moral actions to take their specification from their circumstances, especially their end, more than from the substance itself; and so all such common actions may be holy to the Lord; and that place of St. Peter is to be thus understood, " Be ye holy in all manner of conversation," 1 Pet. i. 15; in all the turnings of your lives, even in common actions; this being the nature of holiness in the general, both as in God and in our actions.

There is a double holiness required in every man. 1. A giving up a man's self to the Lord; "as they," it is said, "first gave themselves to the Lord," 2 Cor. viii. 5. To give a man's self up as a sacrifice to the Lord, that is, the holiness of a man; and, when any thing is sacrificed, it is given up to the use of the Lord, to whom it is sacrificed. 2. A giving up all things, with himself; his understanding, will, thoughts, affections, life, liberty, credit, goods, all his power and might, whereby he is able to do anything; —to resign all these to the Lord, and by so doing he sanctifies the Lord; this is the holiness of a man, to do all for the Lord only. So that the reason is clear; let a man do what he will, keep the sabbath, pray, &c., if there be not this holiness in his heart, all his labour is lost; for " without holiness no man shall see the Lord." Nothing is holy, except it be given up to the Lord alone, excluding self and the creature.

Is all our labour lost, unless we seek God's face, though a man go ever so far? then there is great reason to examine ourselves, whether we seek the Lord for himself or not; seeing that otherwise all your labour is lost, for then you do not set up God for your God in your hearts, but something else, namely, that which you seek besides him: as in marriage, when a man marries a woman, not out of love to her person, but for riches, we say, that he marries not the woman, but her wealth; so it is here.

And then, again, if you do not hold out, all your labour will be lost. Though a man hath been righteous all his days, yet, if he fall from God, all his righteousness shall be forgotten, Ezek. xviii. 26: and a man that seeks not the Lord for himself will fall away, as appears by that scripture, " They return, but not to the Most High," Hos. vii. 16. They are like a deceitful bow; that is, when a man turns to the Lord, but not for himself, he will return again, and start aside like a broken bow; for, if he attain those ends for which he sought the Lord, his seeking is at an end. See this in Amaziah, 2 Chron. xxv.; he went far in obedience, but yet he did not seek the Lord in it; he was content to lose a hundred talents, and to send back the Israelites he had hired therewith, which was such a trial as even a good man might have failed in it, yet he did not seek the Lord in this. He was persuaded that if he had taken the Israelites along with him he should have lost the battle, which was his chief end in that action; he believed the prophet so far, and thus sought his safety alone, and, because he sought not the Lord, therefore he held not out; but when he was put to other trials, to new temptations, and saw another worship, he left the Lord, and started aside like a deceitful bow. Many brought up in good families, when they come into new company and trials, fall away, because they sought not the Lord himself.

Further: if you do not seek the Lord for himself, you do not love him, and then all your labour is lost: for all the promises are made to those that love God.

But men will be ready to say, We do seek the Lord's face. Therefore I will give you rules to distinguish, and to help men to discern whether they seek the Lord or not.

Rule 1. Consider what opinion thou hast of thyself. Every man that is regenerate, at his regeneration changeth his opinion of himself; as St. Paul, "It is no more I, but sin that dwelleth in me," Rom. vii. 17. Before he was regenerated, sin was himself; but, now there was a new master come into the house, that renewed-self, the regenerate part, and that which before was wholly himself, he now speaks of as one crept in, as of an inmate that should not be there. Now, if thou reckonest the regenerate part thyself, then thou hast sought the Lord's presence; for that part is thereby strengthened. The perfection of this self stands in conjunction with the Lord, and so seeks him; but, if thou accountest thy flesh to be thyself, it is impossible thou shouldest seek God aright, for God and it are contraries. A regenerate man says, "Let me have God, and whatever I lose, whether life, liberty, yet myself is safe." He still considers chiefly, Whether doth this tend, to the safety of myself or not? though he is content, and would have the outward man do well too: as if have a fair house to dwell in, I would have it safe; yet if it be set on fire, it is not of such great matter, as being myself kept safe. Take a man who has clothes on, if he can keep his clothes whole, it is well; but if they be rent, and his body be saved, he cares not: so where the regenerate part is, the self, if the outward man can be kept safe, it is well, he had rather have it so; however, if the regenerate part be safe, he cares not much, for he accounts it but as the rending of his clothes. But take another man in his natural state, he thinks thus with himself, "I must not destroy myself; I would keep a good conscience, but not so as to destroy myself." It is impossible that what a man reckons himself he should suffer to be destroyed; therefore, when discredit or imprisonment comes, they are reckoned wounds given to himself; he lets God go, to defend and save himself harmless. All this difference comes from the difference of opinion that a man hath of what is himself.

But how shall I know what opinion I have of myself?

(1.) Consider wherein thou desirest to excel. All

things desire to have that excellency which is proper to themselves: every creature desires to build up itself. If, therefore, thou desirest to excel in things that belong to the outward man, to build up thyself in learning, credit, and wealth, and outward conveniences, then thy outward man and flesh is thyself: but if thou seekest an inward excellency, not caring for man's praise, but seeking to have the praise of God, the comfort of a good conscience, and assurance of salvation, then it is a sign thou reckonest the inward man thyself.

(2.) Consider where thou layest up thy treasure. Dost thou lay it up in the regenerate part, and dost thou endeavour to make that richer, and carriest something into that chest every day? then thou countest that to be thyself; for "where your treasure is, there will your heart be also." A believer, though he hath troubles abroad in the world, and decays in estate and in health, yet so long as his regenerate part is safe, and thriving, and standing in good terms with God, he congratulates himself: like a man whose house is broken open, he presently runs to his chest where his chief treasure lies, and if that be safe he thinks all is well. But if thou layest up thy treasure in the outward man, in a heap of outward things, and when these things are gone thou reckonest thyself undone, it is certain thou makest that thyself. This was the case of Haman, Nabal, Ahithophel, and of all carnal men, whose hearts must needs sink when outward things leave them, or if they be put into the fear of the loss of their lives and goods. But a good man under affliction is like grapes which have wine in them when put into the wine-press, though the skin and husk perish, the wine is saved. So is it with the saints in persecution; their inward man is still saved, they lose but their husks. But when a man hath nothing in him but flesh and an outward man, when these perish all he hath is lost, and himself with them. It is therefore good to try yourselves what opinion you have of yourselves before evil times come, that you may see whether you have that in you which will not then perish, but be kept safe and sustain you; and thereby also you shall know whether you seek the Lord's face or not.

Rule 2. Consider what it is you make your utmost end. We are now upon a point that admits of very narrow differences, for, as we have said, a man may perform many duties, go therein as far as another, and yet lose all his labour, and all because he seeks not the Lord's presence. And the trial of that dependeth especially upon this, what you make your utmost end; for though the actions be good, yet if the end be yourselves, or God's glory be made by you but as a bridge, all is lost. Now, that you may not mistake here, you must know there is a double end; the one of the work, the other of the workman. The end of the work itself may be good, even in hypocrites: the action being in itself a holy action, and tending to God's service; when yet the end of the workman is not the Lord, but himself, this difference runs through all his actions. Two men that go together in the same way may have a different journey's end. God, speaking of the feasts and fasts of the jews, two as holy duties as any other, says, "But did ye them at all to me?" Zech. vii. 5, but to return out of captivity. So there was much fruit found in Israel, yet because they brought it forth to themselves, not to the Lord, therefore Israel is called an empty vine, Hos. x. 1. A carnal man and a regenerate man differ mainly in this; that a carnal man, when he is to do anything, asks, What good will this bring to me? what profit, what credit shall I have by doing it? If none, he lays it aside. But a godly man, so far as he is godly, asketh whether it is commanded by God? is it for his glory and advantage? Therefore consider thine end, whether for God or not, and judge by that.

But is a man bound to seek God in everything? may he have no respect to himself?

The end must still be better than that which tends to it: and that therefore which is the chief good must be the chief end; and, unless thou considerest God better than all things else, thou dost not make him thy end, nor thy God. Again, the end commands all, is most perfect, and comprehends all the rest, and that also is proper to the Lord alone, this cannot be said of any man or creature, and therefore God alone is to be made thy end.

But may not a man make his own happiness his end, and do what he doth for his own perfection? A man may and always doth so, and that upon necessity, as hath been said: only this, there is a double end; the one is the thing itself which a man makes his end, the other is the benefit or fruit which cometh by the attaining it. So that happiness is that sweetness which follows all ends, even as the shadow doth the body. The question therefore is, what that thing is which thou seekest this happiness from, for that is it which is thy main end; whether dost thou think thou canst make thyself happy by those riches and pleasures which for thyself thou aimest at, or dost thou look for all thy happiness from the Lord alone? What a man looks for his happiness from, that he makes his chief end: if from God, then he makes God his utmost end, so that his own happiness is but the fruit that ariseth out of, and accompanies, his seeking him.

But may not a man provide for himself? True, but thus: whereas all that a man's mind is to be taken up about, is either work or wages; if it be work, thou must do it to God alone, whose servant thou art; if it be matter of wages, as are the things belonging to thy name and estate, these in like manner thou art to look for from God alone. All a man's employment is taken up either in doing all for God, or receiving all from God; and, if any man were an entire servant to another man, he then ought to have an eye only to his master in matter of work, and to no other, and also to take what wages his master will allow him for that work, and no more; he ought to resolve all into his master. But no creature is an entire servant unto another creature; but we are so to God, and therefore we ought both to do all the work we do for God, and also, for matter of wages, to take all from him, and to depend upon his providence; so that this provision for a man is but to cast a man's self upon the Lord, it being not our work to provide for ourselves, but the Lord's. Let us do all for him, and it belongs to him to give us wages, and he will do it.

But may not a man in his actions have an eye to God, and himself also? For answer to this, look to that place, " The light of the body is the eye; if therefore thine eye be single, thy whole body shall be full of light," Matt. vi. 22. It is a single eye, which looks on a single object, upon one object only; and therefore a man is then said to have a single eye when he looks upon the Lord alone, when nothing else is made his god. He looks not on riches, nor anything else as his god: and then all the body is light; that is, all the conversation is good, and he sees whither he goes; but if the eye be evil, that is, by the rule of opposition, if it be double, (for that is a rule of interpreting Scripture, to open the meaning of phrases by what is opposed to them,) then it is a wicked eye; that is, if it be partly set upon God, and partly on a man's self, it is wicked. And so St. James hath it; he calls such an one "a double-minded man," who is "unstable in all his ways." When a man hath partly an eye to the world and himself, and partly to God, he is as one distracted between two ways, he knows not which to take; he is unstable, like a drunken man that staggers in all he doth, being now on one side, now for God; and now on another side, for himself: and so his whole body is dark; that is, his whole conversation is wicked, as being out of his way; he sees not a right path to walk in, he hath not a right view whither he should tend, he is not able to see a right object; but he goes hither and thither, from one thing to another, and is unstable in all his ways.

But you will say, the holiest man that is hath some eye to himself in his actions. It is one thing, when a man hath chosen the Lord as his end, and the way that leads to him, though he waver in it, and misseth somewhat of the evenness of his ways, and hath falls in it; and another thing, to be distracted between two ways, sometimes choosing one way, and sometimes another, as a carnal man doth. One that is resolved to go in this way, though with much unevenness, may fall, and have many mistakes in the way; he may have too many lookings to himself, but yet he hath chosen the Lord and follows him; and this is the difference between him and the other who hath two ways, and is distracted between them.

Use 1. But now the main question is, How shall

we know whether we make the Lord our utmost end or not?

There are these rules to help you in it.

Rule 1. The utmost end gives rules to a man's whole life; all other ends do it but in some particular actions, but the utmost end doth command all in a man, all his ways and actions; therefore then thou makest the Lord thy utmost end when in all thy actions, whether public or private, thou lookest to the Lord. In whatsoever a man doth, in all those respects and relations he stands in, whether he be a magistrate or a private man, whether they be businesses or recreations, if God be a man's end, his eye will still be upon the Lord in all. Now, he that doth not thus make God his utmost end, may find that he hath some secret by-ways of his own; some secret motions differing from and contrary to God, wherein he goes, though it is not open to the world, and is perhaps unknown to himself, or not known at all times; but the utmost end commands all, and leaves nothing out, for the least action is subject to it.

Rule 2. The utmost end limits all the means, and sets them their bounds, but is not bounded itself by any. It says, Thus far thou shalt go, and no further; but there are no limits set to the end itself: as the master-builder appoints every man his work, and the men go so far as he appoints them, and no further; or, if health be a man's end, it sets limits to all the means he useth, to meat, and drink, and physic: he takes so much and no more than what will conduce to that end. But there are no limits set to health itself, he can never have too much of health. So then consider what it is that gives bounds to thy course, that thou sayest when thou art come to such a height, Thus far will I go, and no further. He that maketh himself his end, will be sure to have a holiness of such limits as shall not deprive him of his great friends nor his estate; he will go so far till it comes to hurt himself; himself being his end. Therefore, he limits his holiness; he stays in such a pitch or gives over: but, if God be his end, he thinks he can never have enough of God and of holiness; and though his actions of holiness and forwardness therein overrun his credit and overthrow his estate, yet he cares not, for it is not his utmost end to preserve himself, or that which belongs to himself.

Rule 3. Thou shalt know thy utmost end by a secret sense which accompanies every action thou doest, if thou narrowly lookest to it; for this is the difference between man and other creatures, that a man can look back to his own actions: so that if thou wouldest ask thy heart what is thy scope and purpose in this or that action! there is a secret sense accompanies the action in thy heart that would discover it. Consider, therefore, in any business thou doest, why thou doest it? why thou undertakest it? why thou art at so much pains and cost in it? Ask thy heart, Is it for the Lord, or for thyself? If that will not discover it to thee, look to the circumstances, to the manner of doing it, as, Why do I pray in such a manner? why do I it thus and thus, and not in a better manner?

Rule 4. If this will not do it, look to thy affections; consider how thou art affected or troubled about it when the action is done. Suppose it be a business that, both for the matter and manner, was for the Lord; but, when it is done, what is it thou art grieved at? is it that thou hast got some discredit to thyself in the performance of it? or that God hath had no more glory by it? Are thy affections troubled, that thou hast offended God in it, that something is gone from God in it? or rather, that something is gone from thyself? Thus, by examining how thy affections are occupied about the thing when done, thou mayest discern thy utmost end.

Rule 5. Is taken out of Phil. ii. 20, 21, "I have no man like-minded, who will naturally care for you; for all seek their own, and not the things which are Jesus Christ's." Consider whether thou seekest thine own things, or the things of Jesus Christ; and that whether thou doest it "naturally," as the Greek word signifies, as thy own business: to seek a man's own, and to do a thing naturally, is made in that passage all one. Consider whether thou seekest the things of Christ as naturally as thine own: and whether that be done or not thou wilt find by these three things :—

(1.) A man will go about what he doth willingly. When a man hath a business of his own to do, he doth it willingly, and employs his head about it, and is exceedingly solicitous; but, when the business is another man's, he goes about it, it may be, because he sees it must be done, and there is reason for it; but still he doth his own in another manner. And thus willingly do the saints do the Lord's work: see it in St. Paul; "Yea, so have I strived to preach the gospel," &c. Rom. xv. 20 ; the word in the original signifies, "I was ambitious to preach the gospel." Look what desires an ambitious man hath, (and there are no desires so quick as those of ambition; such a man overlooks all for his preferment,) such desires had I to the preaching of the gospel. The like affection he expresseth in himself, "Besides those things without, that which cometh upon me daily, the care of all the churches. Who is offended, and I burn not?" 2 Cor. xi. 28, 29.

The phrases used in the original text strongly express Paul's willingness and natural affection to the Lord's business. They import that he had, as it were, all cares numbered and mustered together, and that with anxiety, with the same solicitude that a man had about his own business. The question, "Who is offended, and I burn not?" shows that his affections were so hot and quick, as presently if any soul were disadvantaged, if Christ lost any thing, he was immediately stirred and affected with grief.

(2.) Dost thou perform it diligently? When anything is to be done for the Lord Jesus, doest thou it with all thy might? if remissly, thou art far from seeking the Lord. Whatever a man doth for himself, so far as he conceives it to be for himself, he will do it diligently and with all his might. We are commanded to love the Lord with all our might; and there is a curse upon the contrary, "Cursed is he that doth the work of the Lord negligently:" the meaning is not, cursed is he that doth the work of the Lord weakly, and with infirmities; for then all the saints would be accursed: but that which is done negligently, which is done hypocritically, and for other ends; for they are the causes of that negligence. To this the curse belongs, and that justly, a cold, remiss, formal, customary performance of duties; as when we receive the sacrament, or are exercised in any other duty, or in any cause that concerns the Lord, to go about it coldly is a sign we do it not for the Lord.

(3.) Consider whether thou doest it faithfully. For so a man useth to do his own work, for no man is unfaithful to himself; to another he may perform but eye-service, but not for himself. Now, so to do a thing is not to rest in the thing done, but his care will be, that it may be done effectually, so as to see the fruits and effects of it.

And if you ask how you shall discern whether or not you do anything faithfully, that is discerned by what follows:—

[1.] When a good action is to be done, thou carest not so much that it be done, as that thou shouldest be the doer of it, for thy credit, &c.; as Diotrephes, who was a forward man, he himself would do all. But wouldest thou do it, though the fame thereof were not known? Dost thou desire to have it done, though another man do it? and thinkest, It is no matter by whose hand the work goes forward, so that it goes forward.

[2.] Again; what doest thou, when there is a separation made, a partition between the business of the Lord, and thine own credit? art thou then as careful? When two go together, it is not known who is the master of the servant that follows them both, until they part: so, when thy credit and God's glory go together, it is not known for which of them thou doest it. But there are times when our own and the Lord's business will be separated, and then consider what thou doest; is it so, that, because thou art not the chief person in a business, thou wilt do nothing at all? If thou art resolved not to be seen in it, it is a sign thou doest it for thyself, and not for the Lord. When two men are to carry a beam into a house, if both strive to go in first, they carry it in across; whereas, if they would be content to come one after the other, it would go right in: so often great works, both for church and state, might be done, that are thus hindered, or are carried across, because men are not willing that others should go before them.

Use 2. Consider therefore these things seriously, and bring them home to your hearts.

1. I will ask you, Whose servant art thou? and should not the servant seek the profit of his master? If a man see a company of sheep, he asks, Whose sheep are these? another says to him, such a man's; for he hath bought and paid for them:—and hath not Christ bought thee? and besides this his first buying of thee, he gives thee thy wages, and provides for thee, meat, drink, and clothing. And is there not reason thou shouldest serve him alone? Then, if thou art the Lord's, thou doest wrong to him if thou dost not serve him.

2. Again, I ask thee, Who is thy husband? Is not the Lord Jesus? and, if thou art his spouse, oughtest thou not to seek his things? One that is unmarried is yet her own; but when she is married she is her husband's.

And if thou wert not thus bound, yet Christ hath deserved it at thy hands; and both these we find urged by the apostle; "Was Paul crucified for you? or were you baptized in the name of Paul?" 1 Cor. i. 13. There were men among the Corinthians that did not seek Christ alone in their profession of Christ; for one was for Paul, and another for Apollos, another for Cephas: but, says the apostle, "Is Christ divided?" If Christ indeed had been divided amongst these three, they might have sought them; but Christ stands alone against them all; and therefore they were to seek Christ alone. He brings these two arguments for it: 1. Because they were baptized into the name of Christ, and not of Paul, or any other; and 2. Was Paul crucified for you? that is, was not Christ crucified? How much is there in these words, "crucified for you?" We are not able to search into the height, and breadth, and depth of this your engagement unto Christ. His bodily pain was the least thing in his sufferings: that of his soul was the whole of his sufferings. "My soul is exceeding sorrowful, even unto death," says he, when the pressure of his sufferings made him sweat drops of blood on a cold night; and yet these were but the beginnings of his sorrows, which fell on him upon the cross, when he cried out, "My God, my God, why hast thou forsaken me?" Consider further, the equity of it; for did not he the same for thee which he requires of thee? Did not he empty himself of that eternal glory and happiness which he enjoyed with his Father, and might have then enjoyed? Did not he make himself poor to make thee rich? And what is it he calls thee to deny thyself in? to forsake a friend or two, and to some disadvantage in thy wealth? whereas, he emptied himself of all his great glory. Is he not upon equal terms with thee? nay, on his part most unequal? If he call thee to bear the cross for him, did not he bear a greater cross for thee? Therefore, says Christ, "He that forsaketh not father and mother for me, is not worthy of me;" not fit to come into the number of my disciples.

Lastly; consider it is best for thyself. This is the argument which moveth men above all others. For, if thou do it not, thou shalt be condemned; but if thou wilt, thou shalt provide for thyself abundantly. For if thou wilt needs save thy life, thou shalt lose it; if thou wilt save thy credit, liberty, thou mayest, but thou shalt go to hell with them. These are the eye and the hand that are to be sacrificed, and it is better going to heaven without them than to be thrown into hell with them: but, if thou art content to lose all these, thou shalt gain by it. The man that is most forward to suffer anything for Christ and God's cause, provides best for himself. Judas, going about to make himself rich, lost himself; it was his undoing. Peter and the rest left all, and gained happiness. What was the making of Paul but his going from prison to prison? How did Abraham save his son, but by being content to offer him? What was it gained Moses so much honour, as to be the leader of God's people, and to be so great a prophet, but the losing and refusing the honours and pleasures of Egypt? The man that comes thus to resolve, "I will be content to be of no reputation, so I may seek and serve the Lord," that man will rise; it is the only way to preferment. On the contrary, he that saith, "I must and will be somebody in the world," that man is in his downfall, he is ruining himself. Saul's thinking to enrich himself by the cattle was his ruin; Jeroboam, by plots to keep his kingdom, undid himself.

Use 3. Is it of so much consequence to seek God for himself? then take heed of forgetting the Lord in the midst of all his mercies. It is a common thing, that God is hidden and covered from us by the benefits we receive from him; and whereas they should be as glasses and as spectacles to help the weakness of our sight, they prove often as clouds to hinder us from beholding his face. But consider that this is the main part of the covenant, "I will be their God, and they shall be my people." And upon that tenour come in all benefits, even with himself. We do not usually think that we must first have the Lord himself. Our eyes should be, in the first place, fixed on him; then on the mercies received from him: for it is said, that "with him," that is, Christ, he will "give us all things," Rom. viii. 32. Therefore, we are to have him first, then all things else. So, "All things are yours;" but upon what ground? "for ye are Christ's, and Christ is God's," 1 Cor. iii. 22, 23. We must have him for our husband ere we can enjoy the advantages to be had by him. It is a common fault, that men look to the comforts and privileges by Christ, but not to him; he is forgotten. As when we come to be humbled for sin, men in the first place look upon a promise of forgiveness of sins, and say, "If I can but believe my sins to be forgiven, and lay hold on that promise, I have enough;" but Christ is forgotten. But this is not the method we should take, but rather think, "How shall I have forgiveness? who gives it? who brings it? It is a dowry that comes with my Husband. When I once have Christ, I shall have his righteousness to clothe me." "Of him are ye in Christ Jesus, who of God is made unto us wisdom, and righteousness, and sanctification, and redemption," 1 Cor. i. 30. The meaning is, that God the Father gives Christ to us, as a father gives his son as a husband to one in marriage, and says, "I will make him worth thus much to you, but you must have him first." So doth God give Christ: and, when we have him, God makes him all these,—wisdom to you as a Prophet, righteousness to you as a Priest, and he shall sanctify you and purge you from dead works, and he shall be your King, and deliver you out of the hands of all your enemies; he shall be made sanctification and redemption to you. Observe the phrases in Scripture, and they still lead you to his person, and urge upon you to make the covenant with his person; as when it is said, "In whom are hid all the treasures of wisdom and knowledge," Col. ii. 3. If treasure be hid in a casket, you must first have the casket, then the treasure; so if in a field, you must first buy the field. There is a mine that will employ you digging all your life long; but you must first purchase the field, and then dig for the treasure in it. And there are all sorts of treasures in him, as adoption, justification, &c. He exhorts us to eat his flesh, and to drink his blood, and that would nourish us to life eternal, John vi. 53: but, before men can have spirits or strength by meat, they must have that meat itself, and there must be a conjunction with it, and assimilation of it to them, and of them to it; so "he that hath the Son hath life," 1 John v. 12. We must first have the Son, and then we come to have life by him. A man, coming immediately out of the state of unregeneracy, must have these two distinct conditions: he is first to consider who Christ and God are, consider the persons of them, and so choose them as a Father and a Husband, to live and die with. And then, secondly, he is to consider what he shall have with them; yea, to look upon the benefits themselves, but chiefly for this end, that they may stir up his heart to love him the better; so as to say in his heart, "Though he is most beautiful in his person, and so though I had him alone, I should have an exceeding great reward in himself; yet withal, when I consider that all within the compass of this world is mine, (a great dowry,) that Paul, and Apollos, and all the good ministers that ever have been, have been for my sake; that whatsoever is in this life or after death is all mine, and that all these he brings with him"—you should look on these things as motives to love him entirely, and not as mere benefits. You should say, "Hath he not given me all these? sanctified me, and redeemed me, and set me at liberty, when I was a bondslave of sin and Satan, and have I not reason to love him?" This is to seek his presence. It may be, though you have done the thing, yet you have not had this distinct consideration; yet use it henceforth to help you: Say not, I am in misery, and there is a promise of pardon and adoption, but look first to the Lord Jesus, go to him, and take him.

To convince you further of this, there are none of you but will say, I cannot be saved without a holy conversation, and what is that but to converse with God and Christ? All converse is not with things, but persons; therefore, in a holy course, all that you have to do is with the Lord himself, to open your hearts to him, to resort to him for counsel, to delight in him. To converse with a man is to deal with him upon all occasions. You are not only to look unto, and to be dealing with, duties and privileges alone, for then with whom do you converse? not with the Lord, but with notions, with duties, and your sins: but your chief business is with the Lord in all these; and with these as means to bring you to the Lord, into his presence and unto his person. This is to walk with God as Enoch did, which still respects his person, for so "walking with" implies.

Again; no man can be saved without love to God, and that love must be a love of friendship. Your love must be first to the person, and then to the commodities you have by him, and the duties you are to perform to him.

But you will say, How shall we do to bring our heart to this? This is exceeding hard: it is easy to seek the benefits which come by Christ; self-love will cause most to do so. Any man that needs a thing would fain have his wants supplied. A man that is pressed with a burden would willingly have it taken off: it is easy to have your desires quickened this way.

What therefore shall we say, to set an edge upon your affections, to seek the Lord's person? If we had the tongues of men and angels, all would be too little; therefore let us beseech the Lord that he would be his own spokesman, and reveal himself unto us. There is no way to set our hearts at work to seek his face but by seeing him: and to help you to a sight of him is not in our power; and yet he useth to do it, whilst we are speaking of him in the ministry of the word. It is said, "They that know thy name will put their trust in thee," Psa. ix. 10: and as they will trust in him so they will seek his face. What was the reason Abraham and Moses sought the Lord thus for themselves? It was because they had seen his face. Thus, of Moses it is said that he spake with God " face to face." There are two ways to know a man; by report, or sight; and this latter way have all the saints known the Lord in some degree, and have therefore sought him, though Moses in a more particular manner; yet all have seen him. "Good-will," says Aristotle, "may arise from a good report, but friendship from sight and acquaintance;" that is, we may bear good-will to one of whom we have only heard a good report, but we do not love him entirely, and become friends to him, till we have seen him, and have known him, and been acquainted with him: therefore, though a man have a general knowledge of the Lord by hearsay, yet he will not seek his face till he hath seen him with "open face," 2 Cor. iii. 18. The Lord's face appears indeed in the word as in a glass, but yet, till the veil is taken away, we see him not with "open face;" therefore, go to God, and beseech him and say, "Lord, show me thy face, reveal thy excellency to me, by thy Spirit of revelation, that my heart may be stirred up to seek thee;" and the Lord will not deny you this request. Christ says, "No man knoweth the Father, save the Son, and he to whomsoever the Son will reveal him." The reason we see not God as we might, or only by glimpses, is that we do not go thus to the Son; or, if we do, we seek not earnestly. You know how hardly Moses did obtain this, and you must beg hard as he did; and, when you have obtained this, you will see wonderful things, strange things in him, which eye hath not seen. There are wonderful things to be seen in the law, if a man's eyes be opened. "Open thou mine eyes," says David, "that I may behold wondrous things out of thy law," Psa. cxix. 18. How much more wonderful things are there to be seen in the Lord, if he doth but reveal himself, and open your eyes! for the law is but an expression of him; such as is the expression of a man in a letter or epistle, of which we say, It is the portraiture of a man's mind. When therefore your eyes are opened to see the Lord himself, you will see such things in him as will make you in love with him. What was the reason that the spouse in the Canticles, chap. v. 8, was so sick of love that she could not contain herself, but because the Lord had taken away the veil, and shown himself unto her? And so if God were to take any of us into the holy of holies, into the presence-chamber, and open himself to us, then like Thomas and Peter we should say, "Now, Lord, we will go with thee; now, Lord, we will live and die with thee." And, if we were to lose him, we should seek him with the spouse, from watch to watch, that is from one ordinance to another, and never leave seeking till we had found him, as she acted, because she had had a sight of him. As Moses could not have this knowledge of God till it pleased God to reveal himself to him, so he would not give over till the Lord did reveal himself to him; "If I have found grace in thy sight, that I may know thee, show me thy glory," Exod. xxxiii. 13, 18. And so should we pray as earnestly as he: and, when he hath made himself so known to us, that will draw us; and that is the drawing meant, "Draw me, we will run after thee," Cant. i. 4; that is, "Show thyself, and we will follow thee, even as iron the loadstone;" and, if the Lord will but put the loadstone to the iron, we cannot choose but follow and seek him. God doth thus by leaving an impression of himself upon the heart, of the amiableness and excellences that are in him; as when two men are joined together, so that no consideration can part them, it is by an impression on their hearts of some excellency in each other, till which be removed, they will not leave off to love and cleave to each other: so, when this impression of God's excellency is once stamped upon the heart, then nothing can take it off; no accident whatever is able to sever God and the heart, having once seen him. But till this be wrought the separation is easy, men will depart from God upon any occasion. When we are taught of God himself, we so know him, as it is, Jer. xxxi. 14, that we seek him earnestly, and not till then.

Besides, after God's speaking and revealing himself, there is something to be done likewise on your parts: grow into further acquaintance with him; which is done partly by speaking much to him, and partly by much observing him in all his ways. Look upon him in all his actions and carriages, and thereby you will see how worthy he is to be loved. Consider the first action that ever he did, the making of the world. He could have enjoyed happiness within himself for ever, as much as now, yet he was willing out of his goodness to make angels and men, and to provide abundantly for them; and afterwards, when all mankind were lost, and he might have left us, as he left the angels that fell, without any possibility of salvation, out of his love to mankind he gave his Son to redeem us. And, since he brought thee home to his Son, how often hast thou been going quite away from him? and hath he not still been as a Shepherd to thee, and fetched thee in again? Thou hast played many a slippery trick with him, but he hath kept thee, and embraced thee, and established the sure mercies of David to thee. Think also of his wonderful patience, that when he has been so often and so highly provoked, as he has been day by day, yet he passeth by all, and spares thee. Think if any man would ever have borne so much as he hath done. And add to this, the consideration of his bounty, his constancy in doing thee good; though thou art uneven in thy conduct towards him, yet a continual current of his mercy flows in upon thee. And consider further, that if it had been but a mere act of his will, to do thus, it had been wonderful; but it hath cost him dear to have the opportunity to do it, it cost him his Son. And then consider the great love of his Son, that he would give himself, and, though he was equal with his Father in glory, would yet leave all to take the same nature as thee; and that, if he had not done what he hath done, thou hadst been undone for ever. And consider how often he hath stood with thee in a strait, pleaded thy case, and pacified his Father for thee. Labour to be led by all these rivers and streams of his goodness to that sea of his personal excellences in him; and gather an idea of him into your minds out of all you have heard or seen of him. The end of all these acts of his providence is that men might know him by all these. As when you would have one man known to another, you commend him, and describe his virtues. It is good to do so of the Lord, to be often expressing his excellences to others, and meditating on them ourselves: it may perhaps win others to him; however, it will quicken thyself, and exercise thy love towards him. There is a double way of knowing things, as I told you; by report, and by sight. Do thou labour to know him by experience, so as to be able to say, I know him to be thus and thus, and therefore I will cleave to him.

And, with all this, consider his greatness, who it is hath done all these things for thee; the great God of heaven and earth: this sets a high value upon all he hath done for us. If a great king doth but cast his countenance on thee, how it is prized! but that the great God should look after such a wretch as thou art, not having anything in thee why he should respect thee so, how should it affect thee! And from hence also consider what he is able to do for thee. Men know not God in his greatness, and therefore it is that he is not sought unto. Why do we trouble ourselves so much about the creatures, fear this man and that man, and think a little credit or preferment a great matter? If we but saw God in his greatness, all these would vanish. See how the prophet describes God where he says, "The nations are as a drop of the bucket, and are accounted as the small dust of the balance," Isa. xl. 15. If all the nations of the world were for thee or against thee, who would not think this a great matter? (as what should we think if we had even but one nation against us?) yet let them be compared to the Lord, they are but as dust blown away with his breath. If our eyes were but opened to see the Lord, as those of the prophet's servant were to see the host that was about him, we should desire him alone, and seek him; and then a man would be ready for all varieties of changes. Put him where you will, he would be content to have God's favour whilst he lives, and heaven when he dies. And, till this be wrought, he doth not seek God with a perfect heart; till a man can say, "I have many things in the world, but the Lord is my portion, and he is my exceeding great reward, and I can live on him alone; it being as impossible for me to have him without comfort, as to have the sun without light;" so that, whatever becomes of him, he is able to say, "I have lost nothing, I am not driven out of my inheritance and portion; I have God's presence." That will be a direction and a protection to us in hard times, so that we may say, "The Lord's name is a strong tower," and, though many fly to other refuges, yet thither fly the righteous, and are safe.

Thou must seek God's presence in time of peace, if thou wouldest have it for thy refuge in time of danger. Both these we may see; "The Lord will create upon every dwelling-place of Mount Zion, and upon her assemblies, a cloud and smoke by day, and the shining of a flaming fire by night," Isa. iv. 5; that is, as the people of Israel coming out of Egypt had a pillar of fire to guide them by night, and a cloudy pillar by day, so God there promiseth to his people, "I will walk before you, and direct your way in all your actions, in difficult cases." God guides his people by an immediate enlightening of his Spirit into those ways that shall be most safe for them. It is said, "David behaved himself wisely, and the Lord was with him," 1 Sam. xviii. 14. God directed him, and was his counsellor; whereas the Lord departed from Saul, and he erred in all he did. If the two pillars had been taken away from the Israelites, they had been lost in the wilderness; so, when the Lord departed from Saul, he was as a man bewildered in a dark night: whereas a godly man shall have a voice behind him saying, "This is the way, walk ye in it," Isa. xxx. 21.

But that is not all the benefit which the presence of God doth afford us; it gives protection also, as that place shows, "Upon all the glory shall be a defence; and there shall be a tabernacle for a shadow in the day time from the heat, and for a place of refuge, and for a covert from storm and from rain," Isa. iv. 5, 6; that is, what a shadow is to a poor traveller in the time of scorching heat, in those hot countries, that will the Lord's presence be to all his saints: and it shall be a covert also; they shall be under it, as under a roof, like one in a house, that looks out, and sees others in a storm: as, when the Egyptians were beaten with hail, and perished in it, the Israelites were safe. And again, he will be a refuge to them. When they are persecuted by any, whether it be by their own sins which follow them, as the avenger of blood, or by evil men, or the power and malice of Satan, if they run to the Lord, he will be their asylum, their sanctuary. See what an advantage Mordecai, who possessed this privilege, had over Haman. Both were in distress: Mordecai was persecuted, he fled to the Lord by prayer, and had him for a refuge; but Haman had none when he was out of favour with the king. So both Peter and Judas fell into sin; but Peter had a refuge to flee to, even God, whom he had been formerly acquainted with; but Judas had none, and so the storm fell on him. So Saul, being about to fight with the Philistines, had no refuge; God had departed from him, and therefore he fled to a witch: but David, when he was in as great a strait, and the people talked of stoning him, had a refuge; he encouraged himself in his God: and therefore you find it so often repeated by him, "God is my shield, and the rock of my defence." In fair weather men care for no such shelter, because they think they need it not; but remember a storm may come, and it is good to provide against a rainy day. When the church was fallen from her first love, Christ threateneth to remove the candlestick, Rev. ii. 5, whereby he does not mean the ministry only, as appears by the last verse of the first chapter: " The seven candlesticks thou sawest are the seven churches," and therefore a removal is thereby threatened from that city. And this is threatened, not because they had utterly forsaken, but were fallen from their first love, and some degrees of it. What cause have we then to fear! and what cause is there that we should now seek the Lord's presence! and then we shall be sure to find him a refuge; for, go whither thou wilt, He is there; " If I ascend up into heaven, thou art there: if I make my bed in hell, behold thou art there: if I dwell in the uttermost parts of the sea, even there shall thy hand lead me, and thy right hand shall hold me," Psa. cxxxix. 8—10. And as nothing is so terrible to the wicked as that, wherever they go, God is there, so nothing is more comfortable to the godly.

Sec. IV. ON TURNING FROM EVIL.

2 CHRON. VII. 14.

IF MY PEOPLE, WHICH ARE CALLED BY MY NAME, SHALL HUMBLE THEMSELVES, AND SEEK MY FACE, AND TURN FROM THEIR WICKED WAYS.

We are now come to the last condition which the Lord requires, before he will hear prayers and forgive the sins, or heal the land of his people; and that is, "If my people turn from their wicked ways." Whence you may observe this doctrine:

Doct. THAT EXCEPT A MAN TURN FROM HIS EVIL WAYS HE CAN HAVE NO INTEREST IN THE PROMISES OF THE GOSPEL.

Now this point, as the rest, hath a double office. The one is, to shut out those to whom the promises do not belong,—If you turn not from your evil ways your prayers shall not be heard: another, to open a door of comfort to those who do it,—their prayers shall be heard.

But first, for matter of terror to those without. And herein our method shall be, first to know what it is to turn from our evil ways; for, when the Lord hangs all his promises upon these conditions, we have reason to examine them narrowly. Every man is born into the world with his back turned upon God and his face towards sin and hell, and so he continues till he hear some call from God to the contrary, saying, "That is not the way." So that this conversion of the soul is called a turning, because it is a turning from one object to another, that is, from sin to righteousness, from Satan to God. And because there are many false turnings, and many men that wheel about and never turn truly, who yet suppose that they are converted, therefore we will endeavour to explain to you the true turning. Now it may be found out four ways. 1. By the causes and motives of it; 2. By the objects from which, and to which, we turn; 3. By the manner; 4. By the effects.

1. For the causes of this solid, true turning, and the motives which work upon a man's heart to turn him, you must know that there are many things which may cause a man to leave his evil ways for a while. It may be some present affliction, for the avoiding of which a man may seem to turn unto God. Therefore God still complains of the jews, that they turned but feignedly unto him, and not with the whole heart; because, when he slew them, then they sought to him, and then they would turn from their evil ways; but when they were delivered they turned to their old ways again. So Pharaoh, when he was plagued with any new judgment, then he would let the Israelites go, but as soon as that was off, he hardened his heart, and would not let them go.

As also, a second cause to move men to turn may be some present convenience. This doth appear in many of those that applied themselves to Christ: some did it for the loaves, and some for their convenient living; some for the hope of an earthly kingdom, which they thought he would have brought; but these all left him afterwards. There are many such false motives, but the only true motives are taken from the apprehension of eternal life and eternal death: the conversion is not right till then, and the reason is, because all other motives may be overbalanced; but the motives of life and death cannot be overbalanced by anything; but these exceed all that Satan, or the world, or the flesh can suggest. Therefore, a man is then turned when the Lord shall enlarge his thoughts to see the vastness of these two; for then all those other things appear but as candles in the sunshine. So that if Satan come with earthly honours and pleasures in his hand, the answer will be easy; "But what are these to eternal death and everlasting life?" These are not thought of by carnal men. Though they talk of heaven and hell, yet they see not the immense vastness and latitude of them, and therefore go on so confidently. Hence Christ, when he sends forth his disciples to convert men, bids them say, "He that believeth shall be saved, but he that believeth not shall be damned," Mark xvi. 16. Where we see that the motives which ministers are to use by Christ's direction are, eternal life and death. Thus St. Paul, endeavouring to convert Felix, told him of the judgment to come, which made him tremble: and Christ told the woman of Samaria of that well of water which springs up to everlasting life. Consider therefore whether or not thou ever hadst a true apprehension of these, without which a man cannot be thoroughly wrought upon; which apprehension, if true, hath these conditions in it:—

(1.) It must be an apprehension of them as present; for a man may have a slight thought of eternal life and death, he may look upon them as things absent and afar off; but, when they are set on by God, a man is pursued and brought into straits by the apprehensions of them, so that he hath no rest till he is translated into another condition. A carnal man on his death-bed, having an actual apprehension of hell as present, is strangely affected. Now, at conversion, the apprehension of these seizes upon a man by a work of the Spirit, and compasses him about so that he cannot shake it off till he turns to God. The wise man sees the plague beforehand, even as present; and therefore stays not till it comes, but turns in the time of youth, health, and strength.

(2.) It must be a deep, fixed, and settled apprehension; for sometimes a man that shall never be saved may be moved with the present apprehension of eternal death and eternal life, but it is as a storm soon blown over; but in him that shall be saved it is set on by the Holy Spirit, and such an impression is made as will never wear out, but he still remembers it; and this is that true apprehension which moves to repentance.

But some will say, " Can a man be wrought upon by the mere apprehensions of eternal life and death to turn from his evil ways, without an apprehension of sin and grace ?" I answer, When a man hath a true apprehension of eternal life and death, he comes to know what sin and grace are, and never before. Till a man considers eternal death, he looks on sin as a trifle, as a thing of nought; but it is this apprehension which helps to present sin in its lively colours; and so also the value of grace is then understood when it is apprehended as drawing with it everlasting happiness

2. The second thing is the consideration of the objects. There is no true turning, except it be from Satan, and the creature, and your own selves, to God. Of this you read in Acts xxvi. 18, that St. Paul was sent " to open their eyes, and to turn them from darkness to light, and from the power of Satan unto God." You see there the objects of true turning; and this is especially to be marked: for, if there be no more than

a turning from misery to happiness, it is not found
If you look upon sin and misery, grace and happiness,
as in themselves, without respect to God, you do but
turn upon your own hinges: as axletrees you go but
different ways to the same centre that other wicked
men go unto, so long as you look only at the misery
and the happiness of self alone, which is the centre
of all mankind. Therefore, in a true conversion, these
motives are looked upon in relation to God, as thus:
"If I follow myself and the creature, they are never
able to save me; but, if I apply myself to Him that
hath the keys of life and death, I shall be happy in
him for ever; therefore henceforth I will forsake Satan
and every creature, and apply myself only to the
Lord." And upon this ground a man makes the resolution with himself: "I will forsake Satan, and
subject myself to God; for he only is the Author of
true happiness."

In Hos. vii. 16 it is said, "They return, but
not to the Most High." There is a turning mentioned, and one would think in a special manner;
for they fasted, they prayed; but this was no turning
to God; and why? "because you have turned but
from misery, and sought your own happiness, and ye
have forgotten me, saith the Lord, who am the
Most High, and only able to deliver and save you."
And therefore their turning was not true, which will
not hold, but will start aside like a deceitful bow.

3. For the manner of turning as it is expressed in
Scripture, you must "turn to the Lord with all your
heart, and all your soul;" though it is not expressed
here, yet it is to be understood, "If my people turn
from their wicked ways with their whole hearts."

But what is this turning with a man's whole
heart? A man is said to turn with his whole heart

when he is fully enlightened and convinced in his understanding of the evil of a thing, and thereupon doth make a full resolution to forsake it. If a man be going out of the way, and another man come and tell him he is not in the way which will lead him to his journey's end; if he be fully persuaded of this, he will return, and that with all his heart, as we use to say, when we do a thing willingly: so it is here; if a man be fully persuaded that sin is the cause of all misery, and God of happiness, he turns to God with his whole heart. Now, unless it be with the whole heart, this turning is but feigned, as appears by Jer. iii. 10, " And yet for all this her treacherous sister Judah hath not turned unto me with her whole heart, but feignedly, saith the Lord ;" which falls out when men have some motives to move them, but not enough; they are not fully convinced, and so they turn but by halves. When therefore the illumination is perfect and full, that these ways wherein he walks will bring him to misery, and the contrary to happiness, then a man turns with his whole heart. And, because turning thus with the whole heart follows full conviction, therefore the apostle doth express this turning by the phrase of opening the eyes; " To open their eyes, and to turn them from darkness to light," Acts xxvi. 18; that is, every man goes on in his ways of sinning, till his eyes are opened, to see the thing which he saw not before. God many times meets men in the midst of their ways, and gives them some light and means, as some exhortations and motions to good, some checks for their evil ways; and, if those admonitions be so far effectual as to open their eyes, that is, to convince and persuade them that the way they go in leads to eternal misery, then do they turn, and are willing to do so. And therefore, when God will not heal and convert a people, he suffers not their eyes to be opened; as in Isa. vi. 10, "Make the heart of this people fat, and make their ears heavy, and shut their eyes; lest they see with their eyes, and hear with their ears, and understand with their heart, and convert, and be healed." Where we see that the first chain of our conversion is the opening of the eyes, the second chain is the opening of the heart, the third is to be converted and healed; and the two former will draw on the latter: and, because the Lord is resolved not to heal them, therefore their eyes must be shut up. But at conversion men's eyes are opened to see sin coming against them, even as an enemy with a sword in his hand, and to see the riches of the inheritance of the saints, which neither the eyes of natural men have seen, nor their ears heard, nor their hearts understood. And then is a man turned from his evil ways, and not before. A man goes on in a course of sinning, as Balaam did in his way; he met an angel with a drawn sword, but saw him not at the first; but, as soon as his eyes were opened, there needed no more persuasions to move him to turn: so a wicked man goes on in a way wherein he runs upon the sword's point, and he sees it not; but when his eyes are opened to see it, then he turns back; and when they are thus turning back, like the prophet's servant, who, seeing an army coming against his master Elisha, they cry out, "Alas! how shall we do? and Elisha answered, Fear not: for they that be with us are more than they that be with them." And so the prophet's servant saw when God opened his eyes, 2 Kings vi. 15—17. So do men when they enter upon a new course, they meet with many oppositions and dangers in the way, which make them cry, Alas, what shall we do? Then God openeth their eyes, and they see also more with them than against them: they see the glorious privileges that they have, and the strength that they received from God: these things encourage them, that they go on resolutely, because that the latter are far greater than the former.

4. To find out what this true turning unto God is we must consider the effects of it: now, if a man be turned, he will find these three effects wrought in him.

(1.) Those evil ways of sin, and those corruptions which before did dwell in his heart, and had the rule there, are now put out of possession, and the contrary grace is made master of the house; so that he can say with the apostle, "It is no more I, but sin that dwelleth in me," Rom. vii. 17 : that is, sin formerly was the master of the house, and that which I now call myself at that time had no existence in me; but now the case is altered, the regenerate part that is in me is master, and, though sin thrusts in and dwells there also, yet it is but an intruder. Every lust is thrust out; and if any creep in, it is by one of these ways: either stealing in, as a thief by night, when they do not watch and see it; or, it breaks in by violence, taking the advantage of some strange passion, so as they are not able to resist it. Yet sin dwells not there as master, for it is expelled as soon as the rebel is found, as soon as strength is recovered; so that possession is still kept by grace : like as it is said of peace, " Let the peace of God rule in your hearts;" that is, though you be ready to fall out with your brethren, yet let not malice rule, but peace. Now, what is said of one grace is true of all. So then examine thyself, how comes sin into thee? comes it in by stealth, or by violence only? When it is come in, does it continue master? if so, thou art not turned to God; for if thou wert truly turned to God, though sin did creep in as a thief, yet thou wouldst not suffer it to take possession of the house, but you would cast it forth; and if it did break in by violence, yet, when thou hadst recovered thy strength, when thou hadst got the hill, that is, the upper hand, thou wouldst keep it under.

(2.) The second effect is, that when a man hath thrust out sin, then he hates it. He that is turned hates sin; hates it as truly as ever he did love it before. There is none but the regenerate man that truly hates sin. Suppose a man hath lived a long time in some sin, he may sometimes thrust it out of doors; and, by a resolution upon some grounds, bar the door against it, as when he lies on his sick bed, or is in some great affliction; but this does not prove that he hates it.

You will say, How shall we know that? I answer, True hatred of sin is implacable, and continues for ever; a man will never be persuaded to receive it again, and to grow friends with it, but he forsakes it for ever. He will never mince the matter with sin, and say, "Thus far will I lop and cut up my sin;" but he will pluck it up by the roots. Again, he will hate all kinds of sins. Sheep hate all kind of wolves, and the dove all kind of hawks; therefore, examine thyself by these generals.

(3.) The third effect is this,—fighting against it. The truth of turning is seen by a man's resistance all his life; as the Israelites were never to seek peace with the Amalekites, but to fight against them, to seek the destruction of them, while they lived. Indeed, it is true, such a man may be foiled by a sin, but still he fights against it; and so shall we, if we be truly converted.

Therein then is the difference between the relapse and backsliding of the wicked, and the falling of the godly into some sin. A saint never gives over the war; he never enters into league with sin. "The Spirit lusteth against the flesh," Gal. v. 17; that is, will be ever stirring him up against it. All the world cannot make peace where God hath put enmity. A saint does not yield to sin; he never gives over resisting it: for this is the property of one truly converted, to look on sin as an enemy; and whatsoever helps him against sin, as admonitions and reproofs, he accounts his friend; and whatsoever helps sin against him, he accounts his enemy.

But you will say, "If all this is to be done, I cannot say I hate sin, for it hangs on me continually, and I find an aptness to delight in it as before." It is true that there is something in thee, the flesh, to which sin is as suitable as ever it was; hence the aptness to entertain it, and the readiness to become as friendly to it as ever. Yet, again, there is something in thee, namely, a new creature, a new self, thy regenerate part, that hates sin, yea, and the flesh also which fosters it, with a deadly hatred. So then, this may be thy comfort, that the spirit that is in thee hates sin, at the same time that the flesh which is in thee delights in it.

If this turning unto the Lord be a condition on which all the promises depend, then it concerns you to examine yourselves, whether any way of wickedness be found in you. If it be, be it greater or smaller, then you are not converted, you are still in the "bond of iniquity;" for this is the apostle's phrase to Simon Magus, Acts viii. 23; that is, tied up in it as in a bond, shackled in it as a man still in prison and bound in fetters: thou art a fettered bond slave; for when there is any way of wickedness in thee, it so binds the soul, that a man is not able to run the ways of God's commandments. Look back, therefore, upon thy former ways; search thy heart as thoroughly and narrowly as the jews did for the leaven before the Passover; search as it were for thy life, because if there be any way of wickedness it may cost thee thy life. Search, also, diligently, for self-love makes it hard to find it out. This point needs application more than explication; the business here is more with the heart than with the head. If it be a way of enmity, having an evil eye towards any man, though he be thy enemy, if thou go on in it, thou art in a way of wickedness. It is the Lord's command, that thou shouldst "overcome evil with good," and that thou shouldst "love thine enemies;" and, therefore, you are your own utter enemy in walking in a way of enmity against others. Is it the way of evil speaking, which comes nigh to enmity? You must not speak evil of any man, Titus iii. 2, though he be truly wicked; for you yourselves were such, saith the apostle, ver. 3, and therefore do it not: to make a custom of this when thou hast an opportunity, and when any man will give thee the hearing, this is a way of wickedness. It is one thing to fall into it against a man's purpose; another to give a man's self liberty in it. It may be done for the good of the party reproved, or when it concerns God's glory, and not of envy.

Again; suppose it be a way of idleness, which men of all callings are subject to; consider that if thou art free from all other sins, and yet art idle, thou art in a way of wickedness. The apostle speaks much against idle persons; "For even when we were with you, this we commanded you, that if any would not work, neither should he eat," 2 Thess. iii. 10; that is, it is such a sin that he is not worthy to live who lives in it. As for scholars who are sent to teachers with a price in their hands to learn the knowledge of God and his true religion, if they spend their time idly, of all others they are not worthy to live. Art not thou the Lord's servant? doth not he give thee thy wages? Suppose it not a positive way of sinning in itself, yet sin will follow upon it. The reason why a man neglects to do what he should is, because he doth what he should not; and therefore the apostle calls those idle persons " busy-bodies," 2 Thess. iii. 11; because whilst idle they are busy about something else, as good fellowship, drinking, or perhaps recreations, which, though in themselves lawful, yet are most unlawful when a man makes a trade of them.

This way of idleness is common amongst men, and mispending time is counted no sin, if a man have enough living to maintain himself. But consider how vehement the apostle is against all such; speaking of the same persons, " I command you, brethren, in the name of our Lord Jesus Christ, that you withdraw yourselves from every brother that walks disorderly," 2 Thess. iii. 6. He gives it not from himself, but it is a command from Christ: and besides he says, he that walks idly walks disorderly, that is, against his rule, which is to be diligent in his calling: therefore he is like a soldier out of his rank, a member out of joint; yea, saith the apostle, " neither should he eat." He names a suitable punishment; as if he had said, " Nature hath taught you so much, it is a rule ingrafted in nature; and therefore you see drones cast out of the hive, and you see stones and all things that lie still continually, that they eat not as animals do." This is a mother sin; it was the sin of Sodom. Solomon often touches upon the sluggard, and speaks against him.

As there may be a way of wickedness by being idle, so by minding our earthly business too much; against such the apostle speaks; minding earthly things, whose end is destruction, Phil. iii. 19. "Minding," that is, being so content, that they mind earthly things continually; whereas men should be so conversant in the world, and use it as if they used it not; buy and marry as if they married not: let it be a by-business, do it as if you did it not. And we should be so diligent in them, as that the best of our intentions be reserved for better things, as getting of grace; otherwise we forget the main errand for which we came into the world, to "make our calling and election sure." This is a fault even amongst God's people, in part, as we may see in Martha, who troubled herself about many things; but Mary left all to hear Christ's words; and Christ, upon that occasion, teacheth us, that he makes the best choice who takes more time from his calling to bestow on better things. Mark the reasons which Christ useth why Mary chose the better part. First, because this alone is needful, that one thing necessary. There are many worldly things required to make up our content. "Thou art troubled about many things," saith he to Martha, "but one thing is needful," Luke x. 41, 42. And again, many other things may be spared, but this is the one thing necessary. And further, this one thing shall not be taken from Mary; she shall enjoy it for ever, and it will accompany her to heaven: whereas death will strip Martha of those outward things with which she is cumbered, and bring care and vexation of spirit; so that Mary's part is the better; let us also choose it.

Again; there is a way of wickedness which Solomon often toucheth upon and speaketh against, "a false balance;" whereby he means any kind of unjust dealing in trading, putting off slight wares with a good gloss. Any such way, such a hidden mystery of unequal gaining, is " an abomination to the Lord," saith Solomon. Is this the exercising of your callings for the good of men? no, for the hurt of them, and the destruction of your own souls.

Likewise, if there be any such secret way of sinning found in thee, as the apostle speaks of, " every one of you should know how to possess his vessel in sanctification and honour; not in the lust of concupiscence," 1 Thess. iv. 4. By " vessel" he means soul and body, which were made wholly for the Lord to put his grace into: take heed, therefore, of any such lust of uncleanness. The apostle means no particular act; therefore, if there be any such secret way of uncleanness, of what kind soever, thou art yet in a miserable state; for I tell thee, if thou hadst any work of regeneration, it would resist every kind of sin; if any true tenderness of conscience, thou wouldst be sensible of every way of wickedness; as tender flesh is of every prick, or the eye of every mote. But, you will say, the best may fall into these sins: I answer, Yes; but they make not a path of them. Wicked men take their walks in sin; ye shall find them there day by day: but not so with a godly man; he never draws a course of sin as a thread through his whole life. When there are ten thousand ways to one place, any one is enough to lead to it. There are many ways that lead to hell, and any way of sin leads to hell, though but one; and, therefore, thou belongest to Satan's division, and not to the Lord, unless thou canst say, "Whereas I was sometimes a blasphemer and unclean, but now I am sanctified and washed." Thus thou must be able to say of every evil way, or thou wilt not be saved.

As for the commission of sin, so for the omission of duties: suppose it be neglecting of God's ordinances, as hearing the word, as it is a custom for some to be absent. It is a monstrous thing that men should be so openly profane, manifesting to all the world that they lie in a way of wickedness.

So, for negligent performance of duties, which will come up to the same degree of guilt with sins of omission, and be reckoned as if you had not done them Thou mayest have a way of wickedness in the way of performance of duties, for God commands the manner of the duty as well as the substance. A man, perhaps, will not neglect the duty, and yet negligently performs it. Now, Christ bids us not only to hear, but to "take heed how we hear;" namely, in such a manner as that we should get strength by every sermon. If thou findest not thy heart, which was hard before, to be softened and wrought upon, I may say thou hast not heard. So, in prayer, when prayer brings not thy heart into order, which before was off the hinges, thou hast not truly prayed. Remember that the manner is commanded as well as the substance.

So, for the communion of saints; we are charged not to forsake the fellowship of saints; therefore it is a way of wickedness not to be found amongst them. What can you say for yourselves that neglect this command? how can you look to have your prayers heard, your sins forgiven? So, for thy speeches; they ought to be profitable, ministering grace to the hearers; affording not dross, but fine silver: "The tongue of the just is as choice silver," Prov. x. 20; and this always, "Let your speech be alway with grace," Col. iv. 6. So, for family duties; look if there be any way of wickedness there. Children and servants ought to be brought up in the "nurture of the Lord," Eph. vi. 4. This you ought to do to your servants; for, when they are delivered to you, you are become as parents to them. There is a strict command to rehearse the way of God upon all occasions, Deut. vi. 7. Those families wherein nothing is done for the bringing the children and servants up in the ways of the Lord, have a way of wickedness in them, and it ought to be searched out. All hearers should themselves bring generals to particulars, in applying the word to themselves at home; and, in applying these particulars, let them consider the doctrine delivered, that if there be any of these, or any other way of wickedness in a man, he cannot be saved.

And though many will be ready to say, We know this already, it is no news to us; yet I fear that if the hearts of men were searched, it would be found they believed it not, but that they think they may lie in some little sin, and yet be saved by the mercies of God in Christ; for if they thought not so, they would not be so bold to lie in sin as they are: therefore doth the apostle, upon this occasion, still put in this caveat; "Let no man deceive you with vain words; because of these things cometh the wrath of God upon the children of disobedience," Eph. v. 6; as if he had said, Every man is apt to think that notwithstanding such courses of disobedience he may be saved; therefore take heed, says he. Such advertisements as these the apostle doth often use; as, "Be not deceived," 1 Cor. vi. 9. It is as if one should say to a traveller, asking him of the way, that at such and such a place there is a by-turning; if you take not heed, if you mark it not, you may be deceived, and go out of your way. Many have lost their ways there. So, ' Be not deceived," saith the apostle; it is twenty to one you will in this particular. We are ready to think God a God of all mercy; but in order to see the greatness of God's justice we need spiritual eyes; therefore, though you know this, yet consider it. There are many things which we know, and yet do not know them, we see and yet do not see them; that is, we do not consider them as we should; and the devil may delude us, saying, "Such a small sin may stand with salvation;" therefore it is no wonder that many err. But to live in any small sin whatsoever will condemn a man.

By way of explanation, I observe, that notwithstanding a little swerving, a man's estate may be good: but it is continuing in it makes it a way. For, if you judge a man by a step or two, you will judge amiss of him: therefore I say, it must be a way of wickedness. The reason is, because a way proceeds from the root, from the frame of the heart, which a man will return to again, be it good or bad; for, howsoever a godly man may go astray for a time, yet he returns again to his former course. On the contrary, a wicked man may be hedged in for a part of his way by education, so that he cannot go out: so Joash was hedged in by Jehoiada, and went straight on for many years. But consider what way you take when you come to the lane's end, when you are your own master, and left to your own choice. And, therefore, because we are upon a point of salvation and damnation, we had need distinguish exactly: and that which puts us to distinguish in this point is, that a regenerate man may have many relapses into ways forsaken; and wicked men may have hinderances in their evil ways, and sometimes turn out of them and perform many duties, and go far in obedience to the law.

The question is, how shall we distinguish this, so as to unmask the one, and comfort the other?

Observe three rules to find the differences.

Rule 1. In regard of the search made for sin. An upright-hearted man, if there be any ambiguous case in his whole life, is willing to be informed to the full; to refer himself to God's word and good men for the finding out what is right. When he doubts, he would be glad to be resolved, and would love him that assists him to do so. "O God, try me," saith David, "and see if there be any wicked way in me;" which was a sign of the uprightness of his heart. When the heart is not sound, then a man is not willing to come to trial, as John iii. 20, 21, whence this difference is taken; "He that doeth truth," that is, who is upright-hearted, cometh "to the light;" but "he that doeth evil hateth the light." The one desires his deeds may be brought to the light; but the other hates it, because he would not have his deeds known: it is spoken of the pharisees, who took it in scorn to have their uprightness questioned by our Saviour. And this is "sincerity," as the apostle calls it, 2 Cor. ii. 17, when a man is willing to have all his actions brought to the sunbeams, as that word implies, that if there be any flaw in them they may be discovered and amended. He desires not that they may be kept in dark shops, like bad ware, but brought to his view and discovery. Therefore the upright delights most in the company of those that are freest from sin, they appear most beautiful in his eyes; and he loves a ministry which speaks to that particular Every one is desirous to hear evil spoken of his enemy; that sin is his greatest enemy: therefore you could not have done David a better turn than Abigail and

Nathan did, to tell him of his fault; or a worse to Amaziah and Jeroboam than the prophets did, when they reproved them. He that would have a building down is glad of those that come with pickaxes; but if he would have it stand, he cannot endure anybody that should offer to meddle with it: so the strongholds of sin being to be pulled down, a godly man likes him that will help him against them. If thou be loth to have it examined to the full, it is a sign thou hast a false heart, and art desirous to continue in sin. It is a sweet morsel to thee, Job xx. 12: when sin is kept as an ulcer, to which thou wilt not have a man come nigh, it is a sign thou lovest it, and art not turned from it.

Rule 2. There is a great difference in the ground and principle of a godly man's abandoning sin, and obeying the law, from that which is in an unregenerate man, who is not truly turned, though he may go far in both; for the upright-hearted man hath not only some present checks and transient resolutions to leave sin, but there is a law stamped upon his mind whereby to resist the law of sin for ever. "I see a law in my members warring against the law of my mind," Rom. vii. 23: this law the other wants. To a man truly converted there is a double law, which is able to guide him; the outward, written in scripture, the inward, printed in his heart; therefore, says the apostle, the law was not given for the righteous, 1 Tim. i. 9; that is, it is not given to him as to others; for others, having no law in them, must therefore be pressed only with that without; but it is, as it were, needless to the other; he hath one in his mind continually opposing the law of sin.

Now, because the explication of what this law of

the mind is will exceedingly conduce to clear this difference the more, I will further show what this law of the mind is.

It is an inward habit of holiness agreeing with the law of God, as a picture with the prototype, answering in every respect unto it. It is called a law, because it commands powerfully, as a law which hath authority in it; effectually inclining and carrying the heart on to do what the law without commands; and, on the contrary, it doth forbid with efficacy and power the committing of sin; and it hath this power in it, because it is the very power, virtue, and fruit of the resurrection of Christ, and is the immediate work of the Spirit, who is stronger than Satan, the world, and the flesh. And likewise, because as a law it rewardeth and punisheth; refreshing the obedient with peace of conscience and joy in the Holy Ghost; and when a man disobeys it, it causeth grief, and wounds the heart. This law smote David when he had numbered the people, and caused Peter to weep bitterly. And it is called the law of the mind, because, though it sanctifies the whole man, yet it is most in the mind, as the law of the members is so called; because, in a regenerate man, it is strongest in the members, and least in the mind and will. This law doth both enlighten the mind with saving operative knowledge of God and his law, and stamps all the habits of grace upon his will. An unregenerate man may, through his conscience being enlightened, put a stop to evil courses, but without such a law as this.

This being thus explained, the difference between a natural conscience enlightened, and this law of the mind, stands in these effects.

(1.) The first is taken from the phrase itself. It is called the "law of the mind;" it having a work upon the mind differing from that which the light of conscience hath; for the knowledge which this law stamps upon the mind differs from that which is brought into the conscience of a natural man. Though an unregenerate man may first know the law, and may consent to it that it is good; yet a regenerate man that hath this law of the mind goes further, and consents to it as good for him. This is the meaning of that which the apostle says, that he "consents unto the law that it is good," Rom. vii. 16. This the other wants for want of light, whereby the Holy Ghost convinceth a regenerate man that it is best for him to obey the law at such and such times, in all circumstances; and when he comes to act it upon all occasions, by answering all objections: the other sees it good in itself, but not for him in such and such circumstances. An envious man first knows what is good, then consents that it is excellent, but not that it is good for him. So, also, though an unregenerate man allows sin to be evil in itself, yet not for him in such and such circumstances.

But then you will object, "It seems then, that the knowledge of a carnal man and a regenerate man differs but in degree, not in kind." I answer,

The want of degrees here alters the kind, as in numbers the addition of a degree alters the species and kind.

(2.) This law of the mind puts an earnest desire into the soul against that which is evil, and after that which is good, Gal. v. 17; so that a man is not only stirred up to his duty by conscience, but he hath an inward inclination also thereunto. So for sin; this law doth put a strong inclination into the faculties, which doth not only repress the outward acts, but it weakens the habits of sin by a contrary ingredient: but the light of conscience, though it may weaken the act, does not weaken the habit. So not only the acts are restrained, but the lusts are crucified; the vigour of them is abated by a contrary desire; a desire passeth through every faculty, which weakens lust, Gal. v. 24. Now, nothing is weakened but by that which is contrary; if, therefore, we look to repressing of outward acts therein, they both agree. And again, if we look to the abatement of a lust, and no more, we also may be deceived; but if the habit of sin be weakened by a contrary inclination, then it is from grace and the law of the mind.

(3.) The difference is in the willingness to perform that which is good, and to abstain from evil. " To will is present with me," says the apostle, in Rom. vii. 18. Men, from various motives, may be provoked to do what is good, but not to will it; and to will it heartily, with all the bent of the soul and the sway of it. " The law is not made for a righteous man," 1 Tim. i. 9; that is, he hath a law of grace in him that urges him on to good without this law. As if he had said, this law without might, as it were, be spared to this man, he being a law to himself: but it is made for the unrighteous; that is, he would do nothing without this; he hath not in himself a strong inclination to what is good, and an averseness to evil, as the other hath. " What I hate, that do I," Rom. vii. 15; he hates the evil which the law forbids, and longs after what the law commands. The law is laid upon a wicked man as a restrainer, to keep him in: he looks upon the commandments as chains and shackles; but a regenerate man looks on them as upon girdles and fastenings which gird up his loins, and expedite his course the better. The law confines a regenerate man to live in that element where he would live; as if one should be confined to Paradise, where he would be, though there were no such law. But an unregenerate man is confined by it to the place where he would not be, and to actions which he would not do; and, therefore, like Shimei, when he was confined, he leaps over the hedge, comes over the pale after profit and pleasure, and dies for it: the law given to him he reckoneth as a prison. Therefore examine whether there be in thee such a constant inclination to walk in the ways of godliness, so that you could even be a law to yourselves, if you were left to what the Lord hath wrought in you.

(4.) They differ in the power that accompanies this law of the mind in a regenerate man. Where this law of grace is, there is not only a knowledge of what should be done, but also there is a power goes with it. This law is a kingdom. A government consists not in word, but in power, 1 Cor. iv. 20. "Whosoever is born of God doth not commit sin, and he cannot sin," 1 John iii. 9; compared with that, "Which were born, not of the will of the flesh, &c., but of the will of God," John i. 13. The meaning of both passages compared is this: A regenerate man that is born of God, hath first such a habit as is agreeable to the will of God in all things; and this habit is an innate thing, like natural qualities bred and born with us, so that he cannot sin: that is, he cannot but resist and strive against it, and have in the end the victory over it; for it is a law within him which puts him on to what God wills. And not only so, but he is born thus, said the evangelist: that is, though this disposition be infused, yet it is so rivetted into him, that he can no more shake it off than a natural disposition he is born with: therefore he cannot sin; that is, it cannot be that he should become a sinner given up to sin. On the contrary, natural men wanting this law are not, and cannot be, subject to the law of God; because the disposition to sin is natural to them; they are born of the flesh, of the will of man. So the law of grace works out all evil in the end; and, if good is to be done, breaks through all difficulties: but corruption in an unregenerate man works out all good, and he returns to sin; so that he says, "I am not able to keep the sabbath thus, and abstain from such and such a sin, I am so strongly inclined to it."

(5.) There is another difference stated in verses 17 and 25: "It is no more I that do it, but sin;" "with the mind I myself serve the law of God, but with the flesh the law of sin." This law of the mind makes a change in the person. Can any unregenerate man in the world say, "It is not I, but sin?" If he doth anything that is good, it is not he; if he doth anything that is evil, it is he, and only he, that doeth it. A regenerate man himself never sins; that is, whilst he is himself he never yields to sin, but it is his flesh, when he is not himself. An unregenerate man, when he is himself, never yields fully to the motion of grace; but a regenerate man, whenever he is himself, acts according to this part, he is never otherwise overcome, but with a strong temptation, and when a mist is before his eyes. And therefore, though he be overcome, yet there is this difference, that he looks upon it as a captivity and a bondage worse than that of Egypt. He is not willing to have his ear bored through, and to serve that master for ever: whereas an unregenerate man looks at sin as a liberty, and the law of God as a restraint, and wisheth it were not. But a regenerate man, though he may delight in sin for a while, yet withal he delights in the law, in the inward man, and that is the more constant, prevailing, overcoming delight. Therefore consider if there be not another delight contrary to the delighting in sin, which yet overcomes the other, though at that time, when the flesh delights in sin, it appears not.

Rule 3. Consider the manner of thy resisting and fighting against sin. And here there are four notable differences to be laid open.

(1.) The upright in heart fights against sin with the whole frame of his heart. All the faculties fight in their courses, as it is said the stars did against Sisera. As, first the mind; there is a change of mind in him; he hath another opinion of his sin. There is a change in judgment, he is renewed in his mind. Let a man's opinion be kept right, and, however his passions may stir, they will in the end vanish. Whilst a man is unregenerate, he is as an enemy in his thoughts or reasonings, as the word translated "in their minds" properly signifies; but "you hath he reconciled," Col. i. 21. And so after conversion a man is a friend in his understanding to the ways of God; he is in his judgment reconciled to them, and becomes therein an enemy to the ways of sin. The question here is not whether thou thinkest sin evil or not, or this and that unlawful, but whether evil to thee at this and that time, in such and such circumstances. Then comes in conscience also, and that fights against sin, which is tender and feareth always, whereas "he that hardeneth his heart shall fall into mischief," Prov. xxviii. 14; and it is that place of conscience which is only capable of this hardness and tenderness. He dares as well venture upon a cannon's mouth as commit a sin; and though he may sometimes be transported for a time, yet conscience fights against it. Then for the will, that fights against sin also, whilst with David he hath sworn to keep those righteous judgments; that is, hath fixedly resolved against sin. He also resists sin in his affections. St. Paul prayed, and prayed earnestly, and could not be content nor take a denial, he was so troubled, 2 Cor. xii. 8. So David, " My soul breaketh for the longing it hath unto thy judgments at all times," Psa. cxix. 20. When a man hungers and thirsts after righteousness, and weeps bitterly for sin, as Peter did, it is a sign that his affections are stirred. Now, on the contrary, in an evil man all the faculties fight in their courses for sin; as Eph. iv. 18, 19, " Having the understanding darkened, being alienated from the life of God through the ignorance that is in them, because of the blindness of their heart: who, being past feeling, have given themselves over to work all uncleanness with greediness." Here you may see all the four faculties in an ungodly man fighting for sin. 1. Their cogitations are darkened; their understandings are for sin, being estranged from the ways of God. 2. Then follows the conscience; " because of the blindness of their heart;" so the word signifies: their conscience, being insensible, admits sin. 3. And then for the evil, they have given themselves up to it; they have taken to themselves a resolution to betray their souls to it. 4. Then for the affections, they are said to commit it "with greediness," that is, with their full affections; such as in a covetous man, who is greedy, and can never have enough, his affections are so large.

(2.) Another difference is in respect of the object, the things they fight against. A carnal man fights against gross evils, as we see in Herod, when he beheaded John. What a contention was there in him! He was troubled about what report the people would give of it, and about the murder of so holy and good a man. But a man truly regenerate, as he is enabled to see more than another, so also he fights against more; whilst another man sees no more than the moral evil and good, and so fights against no more. But, besides this, a regenerate man sees the spiritual holiness that is in a duty, and looks to the manner as well as the matter, and fights against those smaller motes in the sun. All the carnal men in the world find fault with strictness in religion; but a regenerate man's chief trouble is that he cannot be strict enough. St. Paul was a learned man, and understood the law of Moses exactly, and was not ignorant of the ten commandments; and yet, when he came to be regenerate, he saw and understood it in another manner. "I was alive without the law once; but when the commandment came sin revived," Rom. vii. 9, and appeared as a monster, above measure sinful, which before seemed but a small thing to him. So for good; when a man is changed in his mind, he discerns the whole will of God, that perfect will, Rom. xii. 2; before, it may be, he saw the main duties, and the grosser evils only.

(3.) The third difference is in the success. The issue of a carnal man's resistance is, that he still follows sin; the godly, in the issue, still follows holiness, and in the end is a conqueror. Though much assaulted, yet he "walks after the Spirit," Rom. viii. 1, and in the end mortifies the deeds of the flesh. Though St. Paul complains much, both in Rom. vii. and 2 Cor. xii., yet grace sufficient was given him to keep from the act of sin. But a wicked man, though he may have many good intentions, yet walks "after the vanity of his mind," as it is described Eph. iv. 17, and in the end fulfils "the lusts of the flesh."

But some of God's children have had the worst in the issue of the combat; as David, who fell into adultery; St. Peter, who denied his Master. In some particular actions they may be foiled; but the combat is with the desire, which in the end is overcome, though the actions give the believer a blow. St. Peter's sin was fear, which made him to deny his Master; but in the end it was overcome, which appears from his boldness afterwards, Acts iv. 8. So David had the victory over his sin, Psa. li. How doth he hate it, and was fenced against it!

(4.) The fourth difference is in respect of the continuance of the combat. In the wicked it lasts but for a time, because that in him which causeth this combat hath no foundation; like a flower, which, though beautiful, yet grows but upon a stalk of grass, and therefore soon withers; and, the combatants failing, the combat ends. Saul held out awhile, and carried it fair, but in the end persecuted David, and followed his passions without any bridle. Judas was long restrained, and kept himself in Christ's family, but at last his covetousness overcame him, and he resolved to give up his Master to the pharisees. Joash restrained himself the greatest part of his life, whilst his uncle lived; but two years before his death he gave himself up to do evil; "the princes came and did reverence to him," and he yielded. So Amaziah, after he had overcome the Edomites.

In a regenerate man the combat against sin always continues; he possesses an immortal seed which cannot be eradicated: therefore the combat lasteth and increaseth. There was a strife of fear in Nicodemus, and he went by night, but he afterwards got the mastery, and spake boldly for Christ. And so again we see it in Peter: there was a combat in him to his death, as appears by that which Christ tells him, "They shall carry thee whither thou wouldest not;"

this was a strife in him which never ended, till he himself had an end in this world.

Thus you have seen the differences between the relapses of the godly and the wicked, by which examine yourselves.

Observe, if no promise belong to any but to those that turn, then this follows, that if any have provoked God by any sin, let them not think to take up the matter by offering sacrifice, that is, by prayers, and confessions; for God requires this absolutely,— Except ye turn, I will not be merciful; do what you will, humble yourselves, fast, pray, seek my face; God will accept none of these, unless there be a real turning. Therefore, let no man say, "I have sinned, and I am sorry, and confess it, but I am not able to leave it, and yet I hope God will pardon me." God requires all this humiliation, and an act of turning beside. All is lost labour, unless there be a divorce made from your sins. Well, therefore, might Daniel say to Nebuchadnezzar, "Break off thy sins by righteousness, and thine iniquities by showing mercy to the poor," Dan. iv. 27. Daniel doth not exhort Nebuchadnezzar to prayer only, though this is likewise to be done, but "break off thy sins by righteousness;" that is, whereas he was an oppressor, now he must give alms and take off the burdens of the poor; that is, take the contrary course. This is the counsel God gives to Joshua, when he was humbling himself and praying, "Get thee up, take away the accursed thing from among you," Josh. vii. 10, 13; that is, this is not the way to fast, (though those things ought to have been done, too,) that which I most look after is taking away the evil that hath provoked me. Though this be an acknowledged truth, yet there is a false conceit lurking in men's hearts, that hearing the word, receiving the sacrament, &c., is enough to save them. Men would think their state absolutely bad if they should perform none of these duties; but if they attend public worship, give some alms, &c., then they think that all is well. But know, that except you actually turn from all evil ways, all these performances are in vain.

And, to convince you of this, consider that the end of the word, conference, and sacraments, is to turn you from your evil ways: therefore God accepts them no further than they have this effect; "Ye shall do my judgments, and keep my ordinances, to walk therein: I am the Lord your God," Lev. xviii. 4. This is the end of all ordinances and statutes; so that though there be ever so much done, yet except your lusts be mortified, and victory got over those sins which are most natural to you, all is lost. Again, consider that those duties in which you trust, as we are all apt to do, as reading good books and confessing sins, if they be rightly performed, they will work a true change; and, if they do not, it is a sign they are but carcasses, not accepted: without this fruit what are they but bodily exercises, though, it may be, performed with some good intention of mind? because they profit nothing; for the apostle calls that "bodily exercise, which profiteth little," 1 Tim. iv. 8. Therefore, there is a distinction put between a jew in spirit, and in the letter, Rom. ii. 29: and so between a right and a false performance of the duties of the law; the one in the letter, the other in the spirit: the one respects the outward part of the duty only, the other the inward; and if they be not inward in the spirit, and so thereby effectual to work a general change both in their hearts and lives, their praise may be of men, that is, you yourselves and others may think you are good christians, but their praise is not of God. We are all " God's husbandry," the ministers the dressers of it, the ordinances are the manuring of it. Now, what is the end of all husbandry? is it not fruit? Is it enough for the trees to say, We have submitted ourselves to all manuring, watering, &c., but we are still as barren, or our fruit as bad, as before?

Christ will come as a refiner, to scour out stains, Mal. iii. 2; which place being compared with Isa. i. 14, 22, where God says, he abhorred their new moons and sacrifices, because their silver was become dross, both passages teach that the end of Christ's coming is to purge out this dross; therefore, if this be not done, all performances, new moons, and sacrifices, are in vain. Conclude, therefore, that except there be a universal change, both of the object, from evil to all good, and of the subject, in all the faculties,—except this be wrought in you, you shall surely die for it; the Lord will not forgive you, or hear in heaven when you cry, though you shed ever so many false tears.

If this be the condition upon which mercy is suspended, this also follows, that good purposes and intentions will not serve the turn: not but that these must be precedent to every man's turning; and, when they are true, they do bring forth this effect of turning from all evil ways whatsoever. But as there is a purpose which is true, and the ground of sincerity, so there are false ones also. The true always continues, and brings forth constant endeavours and fruits; but the other leaves us where it finds us, and quickly dies and withers. A carnal man may have good purposes, and desires, and resolutions; namely, natural conscience, and desires of preservation and salvation, which two put together work serious purposes: but these are not able to work so thorough a change; as we see in moorish ground and in rotten fenny soil, that they bring forth broad long grass, which soon withers and decays, neither is sweet nor useful; so is it with enlightened conscience and self-love, they produce good purposes, and appear great and serious, but yet are like the people mentioned in Deut. v. 28, who purposed to keep the law; but God saith, "Oh that there were such a heart in them to fear me!" As if he had said, that the soil, the ground, is not good for these purposes to grow in; therefore they will surely wither; there wants a heart changed to afford root to them, and to nourish them.

The next point is gathered from the order of the words; "turning from their wicked ways" being put last of all these four conditions, because all the others do but make way for this. The others, prayer and humiliation, are but preparatives to this. As the end of all dressing and pruning of trees is the fruit, and the end of ploughing and sowing is the bringing forth of corn, so the end of all other duties is turning from our evil ways, and the end is always hardest; therefore, the prophets urge this upon all occasions, "If you turn, cease to do evil, rend your hearts, then will I leave a blessing behind me:" this is the pin upon which all hangs and is suspended. Observe hence.—

Doct. THAT IT IS A VERY DIFFICULT THING TO TURN FROM A MAN'S EVIL WAYS.

That this is the most difficult duty of all, we see plain in the Israelites. The religion of the jews was very costly, having to kill so many sacrifices, and to keep so many feasts; yet they were content to do all these things, but not to turn; they would not be brought to it when they could do anything else: whence appears the difficulty of it. Their readiness to offer sacrifice was always acknowledged by God, when their backwardness to turn was still complained of. Again, we see it in experience. Let a man who hath an evil and a wicked heart be broken in a mortar; lay affliction on affliction, let him be brought to death's door, yet all this will not change him; nay, let God work miracles, not only in his sight, but upon him, yet all is not enough to turn him. As we see in Jeroboam, there was a miracle wrought upon him; although he had his hand withered up, and was by the prophet reproved, and his kingdom was threatened to be taken away from him, yet such would not work upon him, he would not turn from his evil ways: he found such sweetness in that evil way, whereby he kept his kingdom, and without which he thought he could not hold it, if he left that. So all the great wonders in Egypt would not soften Pharaoh's heart, nor make him let the children of Israel go, because he thought it was for his profit to keep them still. The grounds of it are,—

1. Because these evil ways are so pleasant to us, so suitable to all men, according to men's several fancies. Now, it is a maxim in morals, that those things are most difficult about which joys and griefs are conversant, and therefore the chief employment, and end, and use of virtue, is to order them and guide them aright.

2. Because they are rooted in nature, and are agreeable to a man's natural disposition. It is hard to stop the current of nature, which way soever it takes, especially running down the hill: and then, besides, education adds to nature; and custom, as another nature, addeth strength to sin; and Satan adds to all these: for, when lusts lie as sparks under embers, he

blows them up. And to all these add the joining of wicked men, among whom we live, and who live with us in the same courses. Therefore, in Eph. ii. 2, "The course of this world," and "the prince that rules in the children of disobedience," are deemed strong and potent, and efficacious workers in us. What is so weak as water? yet let much water be joined together, and then it becomes mighty: so though sin were weak of itself, which it is not, yet when multitudes, custom, and Satan, &c., join, we are apt to be carried away with the stream and crowd.

3. Because every evil way in us is backed by an inward law of the members in us, that makes it also hard. In Rom. vii. 19—23, the apostle, considering the reason why sin should so prevail and lead him captive, gives this reason: "I see," says he, "another law in my members, warring against the law of my mind." This is given as the reason why he "cannot do the good he would," and why he doth "the sin he hates." And the reason why he had so much to do with it was, because it was a law; and it is called a law, the law of sin, because it commands powerfully as a law. A law implies a strong commanding inclination. Laws extort obedience; they come with authority, and will not be denied; and so doth sin, and therefore it is hard to resist it; it forbids good to be done, and a man cannot do it: so we have it expressed, "eyes full of adultery, that cannot cease from sin," 2 Pet. ii. 14. Further, a law is armed with punishments and rewards. A mere precept is not called a law, because it merely teacheth; but, when threatenings are joined with it, then it is called a law; and such laws are our lusts. If we resist them, they threaten with some evil: as when Ahab would have Naboth's vineyard, his lust not being answered, casts

him upon his sick bed, as if it meant to be revenged on him till it were satisfied. And, as it threateneth and punisheth, so it promiseth rewards, profit, and pleasure, if we will obey it; both which argue the difficulty to resist it.

We may also learn the difficulty of resisting it, from its being called the "law of the members." It is so called, 1. Because it inclines not in a moral manner only, as when a man is persuaded by reason or motives to do anything that is evil, but because it inclines us physically, as nature inclines us to meat and drink. Reason may be put off and denied, but a strong inclination of nature will not be got off so easily. 2. Because it discovers itself, and is most operative in the sensual part, though it be seated in the whole man; as, on the contrary, the law of the mind is most exercised in the superior part, though it sanctifies the whole man. The meaning is this: it appears in the faculties of the mind, when they are set about any action that is good, and in the relation is called the law of the members, because it is discerned in the use of the members: as the palsy may lie undiscerned in the hand, but when a man comes to use it he finds it; so the gout, or soreness or lameness in the leg, though it be there, yet it is most discerned when a man begins to walk: such a lameness or difficulty in our faculties appears when we go about anything that is good.

4. This law of the members is said to rebel against the law of the mind; and, if we will consider its forces in this war, we shall find it difficult to resist and turn from them; for there is a strong faction of evil; many members, many lusts, legions of lusts, warring, so the word implies. It is not a fight against one, but against many. There is not a good motion

that comes into the soul, but these lusts give their suffrage against it, their voice against whatsoever is good; no good intention but they are ready to gainsay it. Nor do they merely say it, and tell us they dislike it, but they will reason it out with many arguments. And they are able not only to give a voice against what is good, but likewise to do something that is active. This law damps and clogs, and prohibits the spirit when it is about any good; and therefore it is called "flesh," because the nature of it is to damp the spirit: as in war, passages are stopped up and bridges cut down to hinder the enemy from going whither they would; so do our lusts fight against us in our endeavours to do good. The flesh so lusts against the spirit that we cannot do what we would, Gal. v. 17. And it not only stops from good, but impels to what is evil; it not only makes defensive war to hold its own, but labours to fight and gain ground, as fire fights with water; labouring to overcome grace where it is begun, and to assimilate it to itself. And, lastly, these lusts are able always to make war. Though the victory be gotten to-day, yet lusts are ready to set on us to-morrow. A lust which you thought you would never have heard of more, sets on you afresh; and, though you stay all the motions and assaults which the flesh puts upon you this day, yet there is such a brood, such a spring, that to-morrow there will be new ones, and they will be still recovering strength and setting up afresh.

All these things considered, it appears to be most difficult for unregenerate men to begin to turn; or for regenerate men to forsake their evil ways.

Use. If to turn from our evil ways, and to resist the law of the members, be so difficult, then learn to proportion your labour to the work, else the business will not be effected. If much labour be required and little bestowed, then that which is bestowed will be lost.

Think, therefore, with yourselves, that if you have taken little or no pains, the work is not yet done. If any man has thought it an easy work, let that be enough to convince him that the work is not yet wrought. The blunter the tool is, the more strength must be put to it. Many stay yet in their sins, because they have undervalued the difficulty of this work, and have thought less pains would have served the turn. Is it easy to change and turn the course of nature? See it by experience: if a man have a natural inclination, though it may be less stirring sometimes than at others, yet it will return again and again; and, if thou usest not as many forces against it as it brings with it, thou dost nothing to resist it. If one come against you with ten thousand, and you meet him with but two thousand, he is likely to get the victory. Thou must not, therefore, spare any pains. This is the most excellent thing, and therefore the most difficult. See what pains St. Paul took; "Every man that striveth is temperate in all things; therefore I keep under my body, and bring it into subjection," 1 Cor. ix. 25—27; he refers to what they did at the Olympic games: they were at great pains before to fit themselves for those exercises.

To bring this to particulars. Is it not a hard thing to keep watch and ward day and night against a spiritual enemy; to keep up the banks against a sea of lusts continually assaulting and breaking in; to take up and to bear the daily cross without stooping; to carry the cup of prosperity without spilling; to climb the hill of good duties without fainting; to abstain from the waters of pleasure when we are most thirsty, and they are at hand; to go against the crowd without wavering, and to bear the shame, as it is said of Christ, who went out and suffered without the gate, and bear the reproach; and to do all these continually? These are no easy things, and yet they must be done; men, in this case, are like unthrifty persons, who complain of poverty, and that they cannot thrive, and yet will take no pains. The sluggard will not pull his hand out of his bosom; and men are sluggards in matters of salvation. But, to quicken you, consider that this is the main business you came into the world to do. And do you think that a little leisure time spent upon it will be enough? It is said, " The kingdom of heaven suffers violence, and the violent take it by force," Matt. xi. 12; that is, he that would have the kingdom of heaven, must use violence to take it: violence must be offered to his appetites and unruly affections; he must keep them under, and that by violence. And, again, he must use violence in his prayers and other holy duties; that is, he must wrestle and strive in them, and be fervent in them. There are some good duties to be done, as it were, with violence. Christ in this place shows, that when the preaching of the gospel came, and the beauty of the kingdom came to be opened to men, then they took it by violence. But who is so ravished now with those privileges, the hope of their calling, &c., that they should thus take it with violence, that is, spare no pains? Therefore, stir up yourselves, and consider what it will cost you. This concerns even those that profess to fear the Lord. Look, what anger and passion they have been subject to, they are subject to still; look, what slackness they used in prayer, the same they use still; their ancient infirmities hang upon them still; they are found in the same path: the reason is, because they think a godly course an easy thing; therefore have they taken but small pains to be freed from the bondage of their lusts, and to grow in grace. So also those without are not content to be at the cost and labour to begin to repent, but think it may be spared, and it will be at any time soon done. But know, beloved, it is not so. Is it easy for a man accustomed to idleness to become laborious and diligent in his calling? So, if there be any ill habit, how hard is it to hinder a man from going still down the hill; how difficult to pull his feet out of the pit of uncleanness, or to forsake any other evil course!

But, you will say, what is the labour we must take to turn from our evil ways? I answer,—

Directions might soon be given. If there be any edge set on your desires, if you were once resolved, even that resolution is one means to overcome your evil ways; but, to help you, take these rules:—

Rule 1. I address myself first to such as are strangers to the covenant. When thou art given to evil ways, go not first about a reformation in particular, but endeavour to get a general change wrought. It is often a rule among physicians, when a man hath some particular infirmity, that the way to cure it is to bring the whole body into a good frame and temper, and thus the particular disease is removed. Therefore, humble yourselves and seek God's face, and leave not off till some assurance of God's favour be gotten, until a new Lord be set up in your hearts, a new end; for, until the end is changed, no good can be done. Therefore it is in vain to go about the particulars first. The utmost end is as the rudder to the ship, as the bridle to the horse, which turns all: going about particulars only, is as if one should set his shoulder to the side of the ship, when one touch of the rudder would do it. Therefore, Rehoboam erred, 2 Chron. x. 14, because his heart was not prepared to seek the Lord; and his failing in that particular is ascribed to his want in the general. It is said, "The righteous shall hold on his way, and he that hath clean hands shall be stronger and stronger," Job xvii. 9: he that hath his heart once changed, holds on; but, till that is done, it is in vain to strive with particulars. If a gardener takes pains to dress a thorn, although it should cost him as much trouble in manuring and pruning it as any plant in the garden, yet it remains a thorn still, notwithstanding all the mould put to it. So, though thou prayest and fastest, and humblest thyself, yet if thy nature be not changed all will do no good. Cast up a stone a thousand times, it comes down again, because it remains a stone; but if it were turned into a meteor, or the like, it would not. Therefore get a general change of thy heart, and then a change in particular will follow.

Rule 2. Go to Christ, and beseech him to work this change in thee; let this be more your practice. This we formally confess, that the Lord only can change us, yet it is not thoroughly considered. When thy nature is strongly inclined to any evil way, so as thou art almost out of hope of overcoming, yet go to God. That passage may encourage us, "Do you think that the Scripture saith in vain, The spirit that dwelleth in us lusteth to envy? But he giveth more grace," James iv. 5, 6. The apostle had been speaking of lusts fighting in their members, ver. 1; they might ask him how they should get the victory. True, saith the apostle, it is hard to overcome, and indeed impossible to nature; "the spirit that is in us lusteth to envy," and will do so; but consider the Scripture offers more assistance than nature is able to give; it tells you not in vain that the assistance therein offered is able to heal. Though the disease be hereditary, and is past nature's cure, yet it is not past the cure of grace. It is said of Christ, "Him hath God exalted with his right hand to be a Prince and a Saviour, for to give repentance to Israel, and forgiveness of sins," Acts v. 31. When lusts are too strong for a man, Christ comes as a Prince and overcomes them, for he gives repentance; and the end of his coming was not only to give salvation, but repentance. Though physicians could not cure Naaman, the prophet could; though the disciples could not cast out devils, yet Christ could; and therefore say not, It is an hereditary lust, and it has hung long upon me, and I have made many resolutions, and yet I cannot overcome it. Remember that Christ cured those that were born blind and lame, whom no human skill could have possibly cured. This course Paul took; he had a "thorn in the flesh," which he could not overcome; he beseecheth the Lord to remove it: "For this I besought the Lord thrice, that it might depart," 2 Cor. xii. 8. So David also goes to God for a new heart; when he could not make clean his heart, he prays to the Lord, "Create in me a clean heart," Psa. li. 10. Think not that all is done when thou hast taken up a resolution against thy sin: to take up a resolution belongs to thee, but to cure sin belongs alone to God. Go to him, therefore, for he hath undertaken to "circumcise thy heart."

The apostle, having prayed that the Ephesian believers might be "strengthened in the inner man," then concludes, "Now unto him that is able to do exceeding abundantly above all that we ask or think, according to the power that worketh in us," Eph. iii 20: as if he had said, "You may find many weaknesses in yourselves, and then do as I do for you, go to the Lord to heal them; and know that he is able to do above all thou canst think, to subdue that sin which thou thoughtest could never have been overcome." But how will he do it? "According to the power that worketh in us." That power is as strong as Christ himself, for it is the power of his death, the power that raised him up from death to glory, able to work out all infirmities, and to work in you all the graces you want. Give not over, therefore; have faith in the promises of sanctification, as well as in those of justification. Is he not bound by promise to perform to you that believe, the one as well as the other? Wherever God hath a mouth to speak, faith hath an ear to hear, a hand to lay hold; as God said to Joshua, "I will conquer those giants for thee; I will pull down those walls which they say are built up to heaven; only be thou courageous and do but trust me: be not discouraged upon any occasion; do not say it is a thing that will never be done." And had not Joshua trusted the Lord, he would quickly have given over. So I say to you concerning your besetting sins, be courageous. None are courageous but those that put their confidence in the Lord. Faint not nor be weary; do but believe that thou shalt overcome, and thou shalt see thy sins all conquered in the end. One word of Christ's mouth was enough to still the raging winds, and is as able to still thy sins.

Object. But here many will be ready to object, that they have striven long, and prayed long, and taken much pains, and have not gotten the victory. This objection must necessarily be answered, for this is the case of many, and it is Satan's way to discourage men, and thereby to tempt them to give over the combat.

Ans. 1. Consider whether thy striving be right or not; for there is a false resistance of sin, and the promise is not made to that; and then no wonder if it be not performed; for example,—

(1.) It may be, it is not the sin that thou strivest against, but the disprofit, the discredit in thy name and estate, or sickness in thy body, that follow upon it; so that, if these were removed, thou wouldst be willing enough to keep the sin. This is not a right striving.

(2.) It may be, thine is but a faint resistance; and a faint denial doth but make the beggar the more importunate. Balaam gave the messengers a denial, but it was a faint one; they perceived his lingering, which made them the more importunate. It may be thou art content still to parley with sin, as Eve did, and so, by little and little, art brought to the committing of it: these faint denials are no denials.

(3.) If thy denial be more resolute, consider whether it be not only a fit, a flash for a good mood. He is but a cowardly enemy that for one volley of shot will give over: Satan and our lusts are not so easily conquered.

(4.) Consider whether thy resistance be not only against the gross act, and not against the least tinctures, the fringes and borders of sin, that do compass the act. These are of the same kind with the act, though not of the same degree. Thou resistest, it may be, the greater acts, but admittest the lesser, some dalliance with it. As the drunkard, it may be, resolves to run no more into excess, yet he will sit with his old companions, and be sipping, till sometimes he is overtaken. Balaam will go with Balak's messengers, but not speak a word but what the Lord shall put into his mouth. Thus lesser sins bring on greater; as a little thief, let in at a window, lets in the greater at the door. If therefore you fail thus in your resistance, the promise is not made to you. It is true it is said, "Resist the devil, and he will flee from you," but the resistance must be right.

Ans. 2. As you may be deceived in your striving against sin, so also about the victory; both by thinking you have the victory when you have it not, and by thinking you have it not when you have it.

(1.) Thinking thou hast not the victory when thou hast it. For example, when thou findest the sin striven against striving and lusting more than at other times, thou therefore concludest thou hast not, nor shalt not get, the victory; whereas now sin is dying and on the losing hand; as, on the contrary, when thou thinkest all at peace, thou mayest be furthest off the victory. Consider with thyself: doth any man but a regenerate man complain so bitterly as the apostle doth? "The good that I would, I do not," Rom. vii. 19. Can any but a broken heart pray so earnestly as David for a new and a clean heart? Psa. li. 10. A deep sense of sin is an argument of our victory over it. This complaining is a sign that we have the better of it: for what is the reason thou complainest thus against it, but because thou art striving against it? We know the mud that lies at the bottom of the water troubleth not the water; but, when they cleanse the ditch, then the mud riseth and defiles it; yet then it is purifying. When one takes a fire-brand to extinguish it, by beating out the fire, yet then it is the sparks fly most about. When we strive against sin we feel it most, partly because Satan's manner is to rend and tear when he is going out; and also it is the nature of sin so to do: and because our light is increased the more grace we have, and the more we strive against it; therefore we see it more, and our sense of sin grows more exquisite.

(2.) Again, thou mayest think thou hast the victory when thou hast it not. The sore may be skinned over, when it is not actually healed, and then no wonder if it break out again. Sin may be only asleep when thou takest it for dead; therefore in turning from our evil ways we must observe a right method. Let thy humiliation be sound, thy faith and assurance perfect: when these precedent acts are not done as they ought, and yet thou thinkest thy sin mortified, it may deceive thee. If thy humiliation hath not been sound, thy turning from thy evil ways cannot be thorough.

Ans. 3. To answer this objection, consider that thou strivest against even a spring of sin. If it were but to empty a cistern, or to dry up a pond, when the work is once done we should hear of it no more: but it is a spring of sin that runs continually; and therefore think not because it returns again that thy former striving is in vain. As those who work the pump in a ship, though they pump out all the water to-day, cannot say that it will be empty to-morrow, or yet that their pumping is in vain because it fills again, for if they ceased to do it the ship would sink; so it is with sin, especially with some sins. Some are more properly called the law of the members, as being rooted in the constitution of our bodies, in our natural dispositions, and these are ever ready to return again. There is a great difference between these and the temptations of Satan. Temptations, as blasphemous thoughts, are but as weeds thrown into the garden, and cast out again: but these sins are as weeds growing in the garden, that take root there, and which, though weeded out, will grow again. We must not hope or think to dry clean up the spring of original sin, for the labour returns upon us as in a circle. As in our houses, so in our hearts: we must sweep them clean to-day, and again to-morrow: marvel not if you be kept in continual labour.

Ans. 4. Again; consider this, that God suffers temptations and infirmities to hang upon you, to humble you, as he dealt with Paul; he sent the thorn in the flesh, that he might not be exalted above measure, but be kept little in his own eyes. Though he cures the ague, yet he suffers some grudgings to remain: though we go in the way of his commandments, yet we go halting, that we may remember the work of redemption, and be sensible of his mercy in Christ. Likewise he suffers such sins to haunt us, to make us weary of this world, as St. Paul, who therefore "desired to depart and to be with Christ;" as also, that we might learn to be merciful and charitable unto others, and to pity them that have the like infirmities. Therefore, though thou fallest, yet give not over striving. It is Satan's object to have us discouraged. Be importunate with God, and he will at length give thee the victory. Christ says, "What man is there of you, whom if his son ask bread, will he give him a stone?" Matt. vii. 9. So if you ask God to give you his grace, do you think he will give you up to your sins? No: he will not. It is God's manner to let his children strive, and to overcome in the end. Jacob wrestled all night, till the dawning of the day, and then obtained the victory. The Lord suffers us to strive long; but this is our comfort, that if we "resist the devil he will flee from us."

And if you should object and say that you do not find it so; I answer, that the meaning of the promise is, not that Satan should flee away that thou shouldest hear of him no more, or that thy lusts should never return upon thee again; but that if thou wilt be peremptory, thou shalt have the victory in that particular combat. When thou hast a fever, if one come and tell thee to take such a medicine, and thou shalt be cured, his meaning is, not that thou shalt so be cured as never to have fever again, but that thou shalt be healed for the present. So in that particular combat thou shalt have the victory.

Object. "Oh! but I am still haunted, and I do not overcome?"

Ans. Strive constantly and conscientiously, and though the temptation may return again and again, the Lord takes notice of all thy pains and warring against it. That which he says to the church of Ephesus may be applied to thee, "I know thy works and thy labour," Rev. ii. 2. Though thy corruptions be too strong for thee, yet if thou strivest, the Lord takes it for a victory. Give not over, but rather think thus: If all this contention hath won so little ground of my sins, where should I have been if I had not contended at all? and therefore I must take yet more pains, that at the last I may overcome.

Rule 3. A third rule or means wherein this labour against evil ways must be bestowed, is to strive to take notice of all the ways of God, whereby he labours to turn thee from thy evil ways; and let them not pass without some impression to that purpose for which God intends them. God useth not only his word, but many other means to turn men; as by his works, and by many passages of providence, he strives with us, all of which should be observed; it may be some great cross upon the commission of a sin, some dangerous sickness, though not to death. Sometimes he sends great fears and terrors of conscience upon some sin committed; sometimes an evil report is brought against us; or he sends friends to admonish us, or executes some judgment upon another for the like sin, in our sight. When he meets with thee some way or other, as he met Balaam, he expects that we should understand something by it; and if we neglect these his dealings with us, he takes it ill at our hands, and so gives us up to our lusts more and more. There had been a judgment brought upon Nebuchadnezzar in the sight of his grandson, Belshazzar, which should have been a means to have turned him. Daniel, reminding him of this, says, "And thou, his son, O Belshazzar, hast not humbled thine heart, though thou knewest all this," Dan. v. 22. This was the case of Jeroboam; God sent the prophet to him with signs and wonders, both in tearing the altar and withering his hand, yet still he went on, 1 Kings xiii. 1—5. And it is noted and set down on purpose by the Holy Ghost, that, "after this, Jeroboam returned not from his evil way," &c., ver. 33; as if God had said, I expected that thou shouldest have returned upon the sight of all these judgments, but thou wouldest not. Israel was carried captive long before Judah: " I gave Israel a bill of divorce" for her adultery, "yet treacherous Judah feared not," Jer. iii. 8: as if God had said, A judgment on Israel should have made Judah return. Therefore, consider what the Lord would have thee learn by all such passages of providence towards thee, which are all as warning pieces before the great army; as cracks before the fall; crevices through which the Lord reveals himself: for you must know that God converts men by his works as well as by his word; and you may take his works in vain, as well as his word. To let them pass without profit, is to take his name in vain, for his name is whatsoever he makes himself known by; as he doth by these acts, and "God will not hold him guiltless that takes his name in vain." God will utterly destroy such a man, for then there is no remedy.

God cuts not his own corn till it is ripe, and all his dealings with his people tend to ripen them; nor doth he bring wicked men to destruction till they be ripe for it, and every such providence doth ripen them. Now all men are, for the most part, in one of three conditions. 1. Some take no notice at all of such passages. God passeth by them, and is not seen; as it is said of the Israelites, though they had seen great signs and miracles in the wilderness, yet they had not eyes to see them, nor ears to hear them, Deut. xxix. 3, 4. 2. Others, though they do take notice of them, yet the impression they leave behind them is but slight, and like a light colour not well dyed, the tincture is soon worn out; like those who considered not the miracle of the loaves, for their heart was hardened, Mark vi. 52. It was spoken upon occasion of their being amazed at the miracle of Christ's walking upon the water, and it is as if he had said, "If ye had considered the miracle of the loaves, you would not have wondered thus at my walking upon the water." 3. But the case was quite otherwise with the jailer; the consternation, which the earthquake and the opening of the prison doors had wrought in him, passed not away as a dream, but left an impression that brought him home.

Rule 4. We should not simply resist sin, and turn from the evil of our ways, but we should fill the heart with something better; for when sins are mortified, the stream of our affections is not dried up, but diverted; therefore the way is not to stop the current of a sinful lust, but to turn thy heart into another channel. The only way to sweeten a crab-tree stock that is sour or bitter, is to put in a graft of another nature, which will change it, and by little and little, sweeten the constitution of it.

But, you will ask, what is to be put in the heart? I answer, Go not about it as a moral man, but as a christian; get justification and sanctification. It is true, it is profitable to be much humbled for thy sin, and you ought to be so; yet this is not the only way to heal the heart: it must be strengthened with the assurance of the forgiveness of sin. There is a double way to get the heart turned away from sin: the one, to see the loathsomeness of that which we turn from; the other, the beauty of the contrary object we turn to. Spend not all your pains about the first, but do something in the latter; the more contrition the better. But it is not got all at once, it is increased by assurance and hope of pardon: when a man begins to have hope, he purifies himself. So it is in all other exercises; it is hope that quickens our endeavours. One who has no hope of a kingdom, does not care about it; but when he comes to have hope, he begins to bestir himself: therefore get and increase the hope of the pardon of your sins. Hence the apostle prays, "Now the God of hope fill you with all joy and peace in believing," Rom. xv. 13. By the words following, it appears to be to strengthen and set them right concerning all their infirmities; and he points to this as one means to be filled with joy and peace in believing: as if he had said, "If your hearts were full of spiritual joy, through faith and assurance, they would be purified;" and therefore faith also is said to purify the heart. And besides, when the blood of Christ is applied by faith, there goes a virtue with it. "How much more shall the blood of Christ, who through the eternal Spirit offered himself without spot to God, purge your conscience from dead works?" Heb. ix. 14. And add to this, sanctification. Set upon that work. Christ prayed that his disciples might be preserved from the evil of the world; but how shall that be done? " Sanctify them through thy truth; thy word is truth," John xvii. 15, 17; that is, when they shall pass through this world, full of evil and corruption, the way to preserve them spotless and untainted, is to have the heart sanctified. When the heart is well oiled with grace, the dirt of the world falls off. This is an antidote against corruption. Though in your passage you meet with much bad air and infection, this will preserve you. But then, how should we be sanctified? By truth; the more truth you get into your hearts, the more grace. Grace and truth go together, and they came by Christ who is full of both, John i. 17. Therefore these two are joined, " Grow in grace and in the knowledge of Christ," 2 Pet. iii. 18. By truth: but what truth? " Thy word is truth." Every truth is not fit to sanctify, as all waters will not take soap to scour: the word is that truth which doth it. Moral truths may do many things in the soul; they may adorn it, but they cannot heal or purify it. " Go, wash in Jordan," saith the prophet to leprous Naaman. There is a special virtue in this Jordan to heal thee of thy leprosy, which is not in the waters of Damascus. You should not come to the word as to a lecture on philosophy, but as to that which works wonders. The power of God goes with it. For withal mark this, it is not the word of itself that doth it; it doth not work as physic that hath a virtue in it of its own, but the Lord doth it by the word; and therefore Christ prays to his Father to sanctify them by the word. As a man writes a letter by a pen, so the Lord sanctifies by the word. To consecrate the heart to God, is to sanctify it; and divine truths alone consecrate the heart to God, and no other. Let us, therefore, get much grace and truth into our hearts; that by tasting of better, the heart may be taken off from the pleasures of sinful ways. Sound joy will swallow up all other joys, such as the joys of sin.

Rule 5. Stir up those graces that are in thee; for when we exhort you to go to God to help you, our meaning is, not that you should leave all the work; some labour is required of thee. I speak to those who have some beginnings of grace: you must stir up those graces God hath given you. Hence St. Paul says, "Neglect not the gift that was given thee," 1 Tim. iv. 14; as if he had said, "Timothy, thou mayest do much, if thou considerest what ability thou hast received; so much spirit, so much liberty, so much regeneration, so much free will to good." So Christ says to the church of Philadelphia, "Thou hast a little strength;" it is a talent, therefore use it. Therefore also it is said in Jude 20, "Building up yourselves on your most holy faith."

But you will say, How can we do this, seeing it is the Lord that works in us the will and the deed, and we can do nothing without the Holy Spirit? I answer, Though the Spirit doth it, yet we, in this work, are to be agents also: "If ye through the Spirit mortify the deeds of the body," Rom. viii. 13; as if he had said, "Though you do it by the Spirit, yet do you go about it." We may do something to draw the Spirit nearer to us; as we may do something to grieve, so to please the Spirit; as we please the Spirit by pure thoughts, so we grieve him by sinful thoughts.

But, you may ask, What is it to stir up our graces?

Ans. 1. Stir up thy light; examine thyself as to thy evil ways, endeavour to see them clearly, and confess them, for that is the way to forsake them, Prov. xxviii. 13, and overlook none of them. With the light thou hast, examine every thing: whatever thou hast the least doubt about; search it out to the full; this idle speech, this jollity and vanity of conversation, how little soever it may seem; as wandering in thy thoughts and eyes, and the negligent performance of duties.

Ans. 2. Use that light further to get reason against thy sin. This is to consider our ways as David did, to ponder the reasons. Let a man take pains with his heart from day to day, and consider what reasons there are by which his heart may be taken off from his sin. To oppose unlawful gain, think of it only as the means whereby a man forfeits all the rest; that what is unlawfully gotten is as the coal that was carried by the eagle into her nest with a piece of broiled flesh, which consumed her nest, her young, and herself. Had not Ahab better have been without his vineyard? If pleasure, consider that it is but for a season, and what bitterness it will bring in the end. If matter of vain glory, that all thy pains taken is lost, for it will be all thy reward.

Ans. 3. When thou hast done this, add exercise to overcome it: as St. Paul says to Timothy, "exercise thyself to godliness; meditate upon these things," 1 Tim. iv. 7, 15. If thy failing be in good, accustom thyself to the duty; if in bad, disuse it, and that will exceedingly help thee. A babe that could not be without the breast for an hour or two, yet being disused and weaned awhile, seeks not after it. Do this against your bosom sin, that sin which hangs on thee more than the rest, single out and do thus to it, as David kept himself from his iniquity, Psa. xviii. 23.

Rule 6. Lastly, observe the manner of their growing upon you, and how they fight for themselves. The lusts that are in us are warring lusts, Rom. vii. 23; James iv. 1: they have a method in fighting, which, observing, you may learn to resist them.

(1.) Observe, when any affection goes beyond the bounds Christ hath set it, that then it begins to war and rebel; even as subjects do when they break their sovereign's laws, they begin to rebel. When Rachel would needs have children, and nothing would content her else, it was a warring affection.

(2.) Observe the manner in which they fight for themselves; the wiles they have in warring. They endeavour to possess the gates, the senses, suffering no good, if they can prevent it, to be brought in that may oppose them; and drawing in by them what may feed and strengthen themselves. For when the heart within is full of adultery, the eyes are so also. They also take away the supply from the contrary side, causing us to neglect prayer, and reading, and such holy duties; as the Philistines disarmed the Israelites, and would let them have no smith. They draw men out with trains from their forts, till they have led them into an ambush; as the fishers drive the fishes out of their corners where they are safe, and when they are wandering in the river, take them in their nets; so do lusts draw out from the Rock of our salvation, from our resolutions, the ordinances, and our callings, and then surprise us. They lead us into ambush by little and little; as Peter, who was drawn to deny his Master, by degrees. They will also come upon us at first with but slight skirmishes. Lust does not entice us to great sins at first; and we, making account of little, and so being negligent, it comes upon us with the main battle. David only looks upon Bathsheba at first, and then he is drawn to speak with her, and then to folly. Therefore observe this, that you may be skilful in war, as the Athenians were, by reason of their neighbouring enemies; and having observed this to be their manner, to deal thus craftily, look about thee, and take St. Peter's counsel, abstain from them. When once an affection grows violent, meddle not with it, have nothing to do with it; if thou dost, thou admittest an enemy into thy soul, that will betray it.

Again: stand upon thy watch, for though thou hast armour on, yet if thou watchest not it will do thee no good: as Saul, though he was armed, yet being asleep, David came and took his spear away. Therefore be sober, and watch; and that thou mayest not fall asleep, keep thyself sober, and endeavour to weaken that law in thy members which fights against thee: be doing something. A law not executed, is antiquated and weakened, and wears out, for custom strengthens a law: the less obedience you yield to your sins, the more you weaken them. When they would have thee omit such a duty, if thou yieldest thou strengthenest them; if not, thou weakenest them. And again, a law is weakened when it is not cared for: care not for the threats of thy sins; and when the threatenings of a law are contemned, they lose their force. If sin tell thee thou wilt lose such a friend, incur such dangers, care not, and that will weaken the force of it. And if thou canst not do it by reason, do it by force, by a strong resolution. Overcome the desires of sin by a contrary resolution.

Sec. V. FORGIVENESS TO THOSE WHO ARE HUMBLE AND FORSAKE SIN.

2 CHRON. VII. 14.

IF MY PEOPLE, WHICH ARE CALLED BY MY NAME, SHALL HUMBLE THEMSELVES, AND PRAY, AND SEEK MY FACE, AND TURN FROM THEIR WICKED WAYS; THEN WILL I HEAR FROM HEAVEN, AND WILL FORGIVE THEIR SIN.

IN this text we have the particular instances in which God would especially hear the prayers of his people. If they humble themselves and pray, whatsoever their sins, God will be merciful unto them. Now, the reasons why he says "he will be merciful to their sins," (for so according to the former translation I rather read the words at the end of the verse,) are, 1. That the Lord hereby might take away all objections; for some might say their sins were exceedingly great, and many times repeated and numerous. But all these are but fit objects for mercy, which triumphs over them all, as a mighty sea swallows them up as mole hills. 2. To take away the idea that all their humbling themselves, their prayers, and their new obedience here required, is required as a suitable satisfaction for their sins. No, saith the Lord, I will do it merely out of mercy: though not without these, yet not for these. There is a secret popery in thinking something must be given, some satisfaction must be made, as if God would not forgive unless they satisfy for themselves, and so balance their sins. No, it is mere mercy, free forgiveness. 3. To set a high value upon this gift, the pardon of sin; "I will forgive their sin," as if he had said, "Remember that you are worthy to be destroyed, and not able to pay the least farthing. But it is of my mere pity that you are forgiven.

So that the matter we have in hand, is a gracious promise of mercy and forgiveness, which of all points else I fall most willingly upon; which will make men come in, if anything will do it. It is the proclamation of pardon that must bring in offenders; whereas the proclamation of rebellion drives them away. Men are more easily overcome with kindness than with threats; it is the gospel which melts men, and maketh them appear vile in their own eyes.

But some will say, It is not necessary that th preaching of the law should go before, if the gospe produces such effects as these.

I answer, The preaching of the law is, notwithstanding, a preparative. In all who are brought up in the church, there is some knowledge in the law that precedes, but it is the gospel that first softens the heart. Ice may be dissolved with hot water, as well as broken in pieces with hammers; so may the heart be melted by the gospel, as well as broken with the hammer of the law. The gospel maketh the knowledge of the law operative; so that the law in its true working cannot be without the gospel, nor the gospel without the law. As to a perfect work of the gospel, the knowledge of the law must precede.

Doct. WHATSOEVER A MAN'S SINS, IF HE BE TRULY HUMBLED FOR THEM AND FORSAKE THEM, THEY SHALL BE FORGIVEN HIM.

You may observe, by the way, that the gospel was as fully preached to the Jews, as to us. So you see it was here; they had the same way of being saved that we have, as great mercy promised and dispensed. Only these great mysteries of the gospel, wherein grace and mercy are displayed, were not opened so fully to them as unto us; they had the promises of forgiveness as fully and clearly, but they knew not the grounds of them, Christ's incarnation, death, and resurrection, as we do; nor those glorious privileges in particular which we have by Christ. For the proof of the main point, take one text; "Come now and let us reason together, saith the Lord: though your sins be as scarlet, they shall be as white as snow; though they be red like crimson, they shall be as wool," Isa. i. 18. The prophet had exhorted them to "learn to do well," &c. But the people might object: What shall we be the nearer for all this, if we be such great sinners as you have even now declared us to be? To prevent this, the prophet tells them, that though their sins be great, of the deepest dye of guilt, (there are many kinds of red, but crimson and scarlet are the highest,) yet they shall be as perfectly cleansed from all their sins, as if they should see scarlet turned as white as snow, or crimson as white as wool, and none of the former dye remaining. And when he tells this to them, mark his expression, "Come, let us reason together;" as if he had said, This is a point which requires strong reasonings to persuade you to believe. Indeed it is a hard thing truly to believe the pardon of sin; and the time will come when you will find it to be so. You shall see how the Lord reasoneth for himself, and how he will make this good.

We will first prove it to you from all his attributes.

1. From his truth: the Lord hath said it; and this is argument enough to persuade you: and therefore having made this promise of forgiveness in the verse before, that he would "subdue their iniquities, and cast their sins into the depths of the sea," it is added, "thou wilt perform the truth to Jacob, and the mercy

to Abraham, which thou hast sworn unto our fathers from the days of old," Micah vii. 19, 20. As if he had said, You may rest persuaded of this; for he hath not only promised it, but hath sworn it, and that oath not taken lately, but of old. There is an oath to it, and an old one, an oath that hath many witnesses: Abraham and Jacob, and all the fathers that have been since; and will he not, think you, be as good as his word? Peter, speaking of Christ to Cornelius, says, " To him give all the prophets witness, that through his name whosoever believeth in him shall receive remission of sins," Acts x. 43. As if he had said, We deliver this from God to you; and not only we the apostles say this, but to this truth do all the prophets, Isaiah, Jeremiah, and all the rest, bear witness. Now, when the Lord hath said such things, and made an absolute promise, he expects you to believe them. It is a greater sin than you may imagine, not to lay hold upon such promises. See how the Lord reasons it, "If we receive the witness of men, the witness of God is greater; for this is the witness of God, He that believeth not God, hath made him a liar," 1 John v. 9, 10. If a man that is of an honest disposition should promise you a thing, you would believe him; and will you not believe God? As if a man had more truth in him than God has: yea further, you make the Lord a liar if you believe not this his record of his Son. What is this record? Why, saith the apostle, I will repeat it again, " God hath given to us eternal life, and this life is in his Son," ver. 11; that is, whosoever believes and accepts Christ, his sins shall be forgiven, and he shall have life. It is the pardon that brings life to the condemned traitor.

2. But though he hath said, this is engaged sufficiently, and this is much to help our faith, yet when

we shall furtner hear and know him to be one of a merciful nature, and gracious disposition, we will go the more willingly to him. Therefore add to this how the Lord expresseth his nature to us, "The Lord, the Lord God, merciful and gracious, long-suffering, and abundant in goodness and truth, forgiving iniquity and transgression and sin," Exod. xxxiv. 6, 7. As if he should have said to Moses, Wouldst thou know the very inward disposition and frame of my soul? this is my nature, to be merciful and gracious. His end here was to show unto us that this is his nature; and this will strengthen our faith in the promises, for all his promises do but flow from this nature of his, and receive their strength therefrom; and he is rich in mercy because it is his nature.

3. Add to this the attribute of his wisdom, and that will also help us to believe his mercies. God, who hath made these promises, is exceedingly wise, and knows with whom he hath to do. He knows that original corruption which is in us, and is the mother of all sin; he knows our infirmities, and what is in our hearts. He who made us knows what we are, as he who makes anything knows the inward frame of it. It is no strange thing for him to see us fall into sin. Therefore after he had spoken of those strange rebellions of the people of Israel into which they fell after their coming out of Egypt, yet, saith he, "He, being full of compassion, forgave their iniquity, and destroyed them not." And why? "For he remembered they were but flesh," Psa. lxxviii. 38, 39. Indeed it is wonderful how the Lord could forgive so obstinate a people, that had such experience of his power and mercy, by those great works which he wrought before them in bringing them out of Egypt; yet he did, he remembered and wisely considered

what ingredients went to make up their natures; he remembered they were but flesh. So the former part of Psalm ciii. is nothing else than an expression of promises of forgiveness; and in ver. 14, he gives this as the reason of all, "For he knoweth our frames, he remembereth that we are dust:" he knows whereof we are made, and therefore is exceedingly merciful.

4. Whereas there is one attribute from which you object against the pardon of their sins, that the Lord notwithstanding is just, and this terrifies you and puts you off: even from this we may fetch an argument to strengthen our faith; for know that the Lord is therefore ready and willing to forgive, because he is just. "If we confess our sins, he is faithful and just to forgive us," 1 John i. 9. This is the ground of all our comfort, that he is just and faithful; for is he not engaged by promise, and is he not faithful to keep his promise? Again, hath he not been satisfied and paid for our sins, by Christ? and his justice will not suffer him to require a second payment. It is just now with him to forgive; faithfulness hath reference to his promises; justice to that blood of Christ, the ransom received, which cleanseth us from all our sins.

5. If all these will not serve to persuade our hearts to believe, the Lord descends a little lower, and helps us out with an argument of his readiness to pardon, from the consideration of what is in ourselves. Consider how you would deal with your children. "Like as a father pitieth his children, so the Lord pitieth them that fear him," Psa. ciii. 13. If a child that is yours, offend you a hundred times, yet if he come in and humble himself, you will pardon him: and will not God, when his people humble themselves? We use but such arguments as God himself doth, and do but set him and your consciences together to reason the

case. But you may say, It is possible for a child so to offend, as that a father will not and cannot forgive him. True, but the Psalmist's meaning is, not that God would pardon no more than an earthly father; but on the contrary, If you that are earthly fathers can do so much, I, that am the infinite Lord God, and not man, can do much more. He is omnipotent, and can do whatsoever he will, and shows his omnipotency in pardoning. Compare with this, " My thoughts are not as your thoughts," &c., Isa. lv. 8. What though your sins be great, and you think them greater than can be forgiven? " My thoughts are not as your thoughts, neither are your ways my ways, saith the Lord; for as the heavens are higher than the earth, so are my ways higher than your ways, and my thoughts than your thoughts," Isa. lv. 8—10. Though you could not forgive, nay, though you cannot think or imagine how such transgressions should be forgiven, yet I can forgive them.

A second sort of argument is taken from the means and instrument by which forgiveness is conveyed. " We are come to Jesus, the Mediator of the new covenant, and to the blood of sprinkling, that speaketh better things than the blood of Abel," Heb. xii. 24. The apostle states this as an encouragement to their faith; and it is as if he had said, Consider how the blood of Abel, though but the blood of a poor man, cried so loud that it came up to heaven, and brought down vengeance upon Cain: how loud then shall Christ's blood speak? What is it able to procure for us? which speaks better things, that is, for mercy, the cry for which, God is more ready to hear than that for vengeance. And this cry is not of the blood of an ordinary man, as Abel was, but of the blood of his own Son. Compare with this text,

"How much more shall the blood of Christ, who through the eternal Spirit offered himself without spot to God, purge your conscience from dead works?" Heb. ix. 14. As in the other part he compares it with Abel's blood, so here with the blood of bulls and goats, which in the old law served by God's appointment for the outward purification of the flesh. We are not able to conceive, nor he to express, how much more, how infinitely, transcendently more, above our thoughts or imaginations shall the blood of the Son of God be able to purge our consciences! He only says, "How much more!" and he backeth it with two reasons, which put together, show the transcendency of that sufficiency in Christ's blood to cleanse us: the first from the eternal Spirit, whereby he offered up himself; it was not the blood or sacrifice of a mere man, but of God; and secondly, which sacrifice was in itself without spot.

There are three objections we usually make against ourselves on account of our sins. 1. That they are so many. 2. So great. 3. That they have been frequently repeated. Now the sprinkling of the blood of Christ thus offered, is sufficient to cleanse your consciences from, and to take away all these. "Then will I sprinkle clean water upon you, and ye shall be clean: from all your filthiness, and from all your idols, will I cleanse you," Ezek. xxxvi. 25. The blood of Christ cleanseth from all filthiness and all sins, though ever so many; and even from filthiness and idols, though such great sins. Ah! but I have also fallen often into them. His blood is therefore compared to a fountain set open for sin and for uncleanness, Zech. xiii. 1; not a cistern, but a fountain, a continual spring perpetually running to cleanse us: so that as there is a spring of sin in us, that as we are defiled again and again, so there is a spring of virtue in his blood to cleanse us, never to be dried up.

Another reason is taken from the freeness of the covenant which God hath made with mankind: If any man be athirst, yea if any man will, let him come and drink of the waters of life freely. See how it is set down, " In the last day, that great day of the feast, Jesus stood and cried, saying, If any man thirst, let him come unto me, and drink," John vii. 37. He makes a proclamation for all to come; as also, Rev. xxi. 6, xxii. 17, where he makes the like general invitation, and adds, that they shall have it "freely." So the tenor of the covenant runs, If any thirst, let him come and take freely; that is, I will bestow it without any other condition but coming, without which no man can partake of it, and thirsting, without which no man will come or prize it. The consideration of this covenant, therefore, should incline us and help us to believe the truth of this point, that whatsoever our sins are, yet if we humble ourselves and forsake them, they shall be pardoned.

Use 1. Before I apply this to any man, I must exclude those whom the Lord excludes, or rather who exclude themselves. Still remember what is the last letter of his name : That he will not hold the wicked innocent, Exodus xxxiv. 7. Thou that art a carnal man, hast nothing to do with the children's bread ; thou art a dog, which may be made good to thy conscience out of 2 Pet. ii. 22. Like the dog thou returnest to thy vomit; for in thy sickness and in thy distress, didst thou not make many promises and resolutions against thy ways and courses? and, after thy recovery, didst thou not return to them again with as much greediness as ever?

Again: thou dost not thirst after these promises; thou carest not for them; these precious promises contain in them most rich and precious treasures, and no one shall ever obtain them that doth not in some measure truly prize them above all things whatsoever: thou, that never hadst thy heart broken with the apprehension of sin and God's wrath, dost not thirst after them, and so hast nothing to do with this water of life. A man whose heart has never been broken, who has never been affrighted with sin and wrath, may hear these promises spoken of, but has nothing to do with them.

Further: they that are hypocrites are also excluded, for they are to have their portion in hell fire, and therefore, whilst remaining such, have nothing to do with the promises. A hypocrite is one that is not willing to omit holy duties altogether, and yet is not willing to do them thoroughly; one that, like the eagle, soars high in fair pretences, but still hath the prey that is below in his eye, and will stoop for it upon occasion, eyeing preferment, credit, or riches, all the while. Thou mayest be white in thine own eyes, and washed before a communion, and such like, as swine may be washed as well as sheep, but yet the swinish nature remains.

Or, it may be, thou art a wicked man. But you will say, Who are those wicked men?

I will give you a description of them, which no man can dispute. They are such as hate the Lord. Nor can any man wonder if he be called a wicked man, coming within the compass of this character, for it is the note given in the second commandment. Many will be ready to say, I hope my condition is good, I am none of those who hate the Lord: but there are many thousands who think well of themselves, who yet when they come to the trial, will be found to hate the Lord. And therefore to try thee in this, give me leave to ask thee but a few questions.

Dost thou not hate the law? dost thou not wish that the law were not so strict, and that it gave more liberty? Let an unregenerate man try himself by this, and he will find such a disposition in him, that he desires that the law would give him leave to commit such and such a sin: he esteems the law as a thing that is contrary to him. Where there is contrariety, there is hatred; and if men hate the law, they hate the Law-giver, God; for the law is the express image of God.

Again: I would ask thee, if this be not also thy disposition, that thou hast no great delight to be where the Lord is? Thou hast not any delight in holy duties, otherwise than as custom, and natural conscience have made them familiar to thee; nor to be in the company of the saints,—for where two or three of them are, there God is among them,—but when thou art among them, thou art, as it were, out of thy element; if they be such as are formal, like thyself, thou canst bear with them; but if they be holy, and the holiness of God appear in them, thou delightest not in them. Thou couldest, it may be, be among the saints, if they hold their tongues, but let God shine in them, then thou canst not endure to be there.

Again; dost thou hate those that are like the Lord? for if thou dost, thou hatest the Lord himself; for, as we try our love to the Lord by our love to the brethren, so our hatred also. Is there a secret dislike of them, though thou knowest not why? an antipathy, though happily thou canst not give a reason of it? It is because enmity exists within: all endowments, sweetness of converse and disposition, eminence of parts in the saints, will not take away the enmity that is in wicked men against them. David was a poet, a soldier, a man of excellent parts, wise and valiant, yet had abundance of hatred amongst men for his goodness.

Again: doest thou not desire that there were no God? Couldst thou not be content to live for ever in this world, so that thou wert happy here, and so there were no hell? Couldst thou not be content that there were no heaven, no God, no Judge at the last? If every unregenerate man would examine himself, he would find this in himself. Now, if any wish that such an one were not, it is a sign he hates him, for that is the property of hatred, to desire the utmost removal of the things hated.

Again: dost thou not lie in some sin which thou knowest is a sin? Now, every man that lies in a sin, a known sin, feareth God as a Judge. Let him be a thief, and he will fear the judge, and whom a man thus feareth, he hateth. He that walks in darkness hates the light, and God who is the Author of that light. If thou dost therefore live in some evil way or other, wherein thou dost allow thyself, thou hast no interest in these promises: only those that claim interest in the promises, that make conscience of all their ways, dare not omit the least duty, or perform it slightly.

Lastly: consider, art thou not one of the foolish virgins, deferring repentance, not caring to provide oil in time, but thinkest thou canst do it time enough at death? and that you will repent before you die. Like the sluggard in the Proverbs, tumbling in the bed of thy sin securely, and, loth to rise; turning like the door on the hinges, but still remaining upon the same hinges. The Lord hath said, that he will not be merciful to such a man, but that his anger shall smoke against him, Deut. xxix. 20.

But you will say, Do you preach condemnation to us? will you leave us desperate? I answer, We preach condemnation to you whilst you are in such courses, and would make you despair of yourselves, to drive you out of yourselves to Christ,—and it were a hour well spent, to put you out of hope. But what! may we have no hope left? None, in the state you stand, but that of the hypocrite, which perisheth with him; for if thy hope were true, it would purify thy heart, 1 John iii. 3. But I may pray? But if thou continuest in thy sins, thy sins shall outcry thy prayers, and at the day of thy death, when the least interest in these promises will be worth a world, it will be said to thee, that thou hadst nothing to do with them, and that there was a time when God called upon thee, and thou wouldest not, and therefore then, though thou cry to him, God will not hear thee, Prov. i. 28.

Use 2. But if there be any broken-hearted sinners desiring to fear the Lord, and to serve him sincerely, who have this witness in their consciences, that though they do not that good they would, yet they strive against all sins, allow themselves in none, whether small or great,—to you I say, Trust perfectly on the "grace brought unto you at the revelation of Jesus Christ," 1 Pet. i. 13; trust not by halves, but trust perfectly. If I had bidden you trust in your sanctification, you might have done it imperfectly, because your sanctification is but imperfect; but seeing it is the free grace of God which is brought to you as a rock to trust and rely upon, trust perfectly upon it;

commit all your weight and burden to it. God, when he made the covenant of grace, took an oath to that end, that " we might have a strong consolation," Heb. vi. 18. This is an argument commonly forgotten among christians, and so they want that strong consolation which they might have. Do you think it a small matter, to take an oath of God partly, or in any degree in vain? God hath sworn, that you might have strong consolation, and he would have it so strong, that when Satan sets upon you, it may be as a strong fortress to hold out against all assaults. Why is your faith so weak then? what are the impediments?

One impediment is, that we are deceived in the covenant. Hath not the Lord promised to justify the ungodly, and commanded us to "believe on him that justifieth the ungodly," Rom. iv. 5, and hath bidden us come with an empty hand? But thou comest with a hand full of thine own humiliation, and sayest, that thou durst not come before, and now thou canst come better in; but the more thou hast in thy hand, the less firm is thy hold. A man that is in danger of being drowned, cannot take hold of a cable cast to save his life, if he keep any thing in his hand: an empty hand takes the fastest hold. Thy humiliation, if true, will empty thee of all self-conceit: therefore, if thou, through true humiliation, hast nothing of thine own to trust to, thou art the fitter object for mercy. Be not always poring downwards on thy sins, but look up to God. " We have a strong consolation, who have fled for refuge to lay hold upon the hope set before us: which hope we have as an anchor of the soul, both sure and steadfast, and which entereth into that within the veil," Heb. vi. 18, 19. This our hope is not said to be anything in ourselves, but is as a refuge which we flee unto out of ourselves, and is laid before us; grows not within from what is within us, but is from above. Now, by hope, we are not to understand the thing hoped for, or the grace of hope in us, but that sure promise of God ratified by an oath; this is the object of our hope, and therefore called " our hope." That is it which is our refuge, and which is laid before us, and proceeds from God alone, which if we anchor upon, we shall have strong consolation, both for sureness in not failing us, and for steadiness in establishing our hearts. But whilst we flee for refuge to any thing in ourselves, or cast anchor upon it, we are tossed with every wave.

Our daily infirmities also are a great impediment. A man thinks, If I had faith, that would so purify my heart, that I should not fall so often as I do; which whilst I do, how can I have such strong consolation? This I say to all upright-hearted christians, that their infirmities should not dishearten their faith and consolation, but they should rather labour to strengthen their sanctification. Say with thyself, Because my sins are and have been greater than other men's, therefore I will labour more for sanctification hereafter; I will love more than others, and be more serviceable for the time to come,—but say not, therefore, I will doubt or despair of God's mercy.

Another hinderance to thy laying hold of the promises of forgiveness, is a conceit of thy want of humiliation, as if it were not humble enough; but if it be so much as brings thee home to Christ, if thou thirst for Christ, so that nothing will content thee till thou hast him, fear not to lay hold, this is enough, stand not upon the measure.

Lastly: it may be thou hast not prayed enough for assurance of forgiveness, and therefore wantest it. In the text it is put in as a condition, " If my people pray;" and, among other things, for the forgiveness of sins, and the assurance of pardon. All the arguments in the world cannot persuade the heart of this, nothing but the Spirit of adoption. And can so great a mercy be obtained without fervent prayer? therefore go to God, and entreat his favour, and though he may defer, yet continue in prayer; for it may be the Lord withholds it, because he would have thee set a high value upon it, which thou wouldest not do, if thou shouldest obtain it easily. But be not discouraged, continue thou to pray still, and in the end thou shalt have it with a full hand. All ye that are upright and sincere in heart, here is your comfort; continue thus to seek God's face, and all your sins shall be as if they had never been committed by you. For what is said of the sins of Israel and Judah? "The iniquity of Israel shall be sought for, and there shall be none," Jer. l. 20: so shall thine be in the day when they shall be sought for. Is not this a great and unspeakable mercy? A man shall be as if he had never committed sin, even as if he were as innocent as Adam was in paradise before the fall.

But, you will object and say, Can sins that have been committed cease to have been committed, or cease to be sins? I answer: It is true, that which is once done can never be undone. All the acts remain as things once done, so that it may be said, They were committed, and were thus heinous; when therefore it is said, "There shall be none," the meaning is, they shall be of no efficacy, they shall never be able to do you hurt. As our Saviour said to his disciples, "I give you power to tread upon serpents and scorpions, and nothing shall hurt you," Luke x. 19, so I may say of sin, It shall not hurt you, because the sting is taken away in and by Christ; or as the fire in Nebuchadnezzar's furnace had power enough to burn others, but not so much as to singe a hair of the three children, because Christ was with them, so those sins, which would sting and shall sting others to death, because of their impenitence, yet shall do thee no hurt, but fall like the viper from off St. Paul's hand, and not hurt thee. It is an opinion of some, that God can see no sin in his children, because, say they, when a man is once in Christ, there is none to be seen. But that is not the meaning of the saying, " God sees no iniquity in Jacob:" the iniquities are there, but as in a debt-book, crossed and cancelled; though the lines be drawn over, yet the sums may be read, yet so as that they cannot be sued for, because they are crossed and cancelled. When sin begins to fall from its proper element and sphere, that is, an unregenerate heart, where it had dominion, and reigned and moved as in its orbit, the influence of it decays, and shall, at length, both in the guilt and power of it, wholly vanish.

I will also add this caution: The saints must know that for all this, their sins are retained, till they actually repent again; the Lord's wrath is kindled against them, and they may feel such effects of it as may make their hearts ache. Thus God was angry with the Israelites that fled before their enemies, till the accursed thing was taken away. So when David sinned in the matter of Uriah, it is said at the end of the chapter, " The thing that David had done displeased the Lord," 2 Sam. xi. 27 ; and this was the wrath of a father against him, but not of an enemy; and God was not well pleased with him again, until he had humbled himself and repented. Therefore, that you may have strong consolation, search and examine your hearts and lives, and see that there be no way of wickedness unrepented of in you, before you apply all these promises, which then you may do to your comfort.

Use. Somewhat is now to be said, even to those whom before we excluded; for the end of our preaching is not to shut them out for ever. The Lord will be merciful to you if you be humbled: here is an open door for those that are without, a ground to exhort them to come in. Come, and welcome. God is exceedingly merciful, and ready to forgive and receive you. If any thing will draw men in, the promises of mercy will: the hue and cry makes the thief flee away the faster.

The proclamation of pardon brings the rebels in, and what greater motive can we use than this, that whatever their sins, ever so great in themselves, and aggravated with ever so many circumstances, yet if they will come and humble themselves, and turn to God, God will be merciful to them. Whatever their sins, they have not gone beyond that price which hath been paid for them; and God will not only pardon their sins, but also leave a blessing behind. If you indeed should come thus to any man whom you have offended, he would say, What! having wronged me thus, are you not ashamed to come to me, to look me in the face? not to ask forgiveness only, but to ask such a kindness, such a favour at my hands also? how could you have the face to do it? But the Lord never gives that answer, for he is not as man; "If a man put away his wife, and she become another man's, shall he return unto her again? yet return again to me, says God," Jer. iii. 1. It is possible for men to commit such sins that men cannot forgive, but God can pardon the greatest sins.

Some sins are small as mists, some greater and

grosser as clouds. God's mercy is able to scatter both. Do not say, Oh, I had been a happy man, if I had not fallen into this or that sin, I had then been pardoned. It is true, that in respect of God's dishonour, it had been better that thou hadst not committed it; but yet this I will say, that in respect of obtaining pardon, thou mayest be happy notwithstanding. If thou humble thyself, this sin will not bar thee from happiness; but thou mayest be in as good a condition after thou hast returned, as any other whose sins have been smaller; and know, that when thou hast returned, God looking upon thee in Christ, all thy sins displease him not so much, as thy repentance in and through Christ pleaseth him.

If any should ask, But how shall a man be persuaded of God's readiness to forgive? I answer, consider that text, "As I live, saith the Lord God, I have no pleasure in the death of the wicked; but that the wicked turn from his way and live: turn ye, turn ye from your evil ways; for why will ye die?" Ezek. xxxiii. 11. He hath taken an oath, that he delights more in saving than in destroying, and you may believe him. Consider also, what Christ was wont to do in the days of his flesh, and he is still as merciful a High Priest as ever: none were more welcome to him than publicans and harlots, who came with repentance to him, and he is as ready to receive us now, as them in those days.

But, perhaps, you will say, I doubt not Christ's willingness, but what will God the Father do? I reply, It is certain, he is not willing that his Son should have suffered in vain, which would be the case if such sinners as you are should not be saved: hereby the value of the blood of Christ is proved, that it is sprinkled on many for great sins. Think not, therefore, that God is backward to pardon, Psa. cxxx. 3, 4. There are two arguments to help us to believe this. If God were backward to pardon, none would be saved; "If thou, Lord, shouldest mark iniquity, O Lord, who shall stand?" Now, it is not his will that all flesh should perish, and therefore he will not cast men clean off for their sins. Again, none else would worship him; "There is forgiveness with thee, that thou mayest be feared:" it is his full purpose to have some servants to fear and worship him. Yea, shall I go further? God is not only ready to forgive, but desirous of it, yea, he rejoices when a great sinner returns to him; which is taught us in the parables of the lost sheep, and the lost piece of money. How did the woman rejoice when she found her money, and the shepherd when he found his sheep! Luke xv. And likewise in the parable of the prodigal son, how glad was the father when he heard that his son was coming home, who had lived riotously and spent his goods! These parables teach us, that God is thus affected when a great sinner returns to him. Besides, he doth not only say, If you will come, I will receive you, I will not shut you out; but he inviteth them, calleth them, yea more, sends his ministers to fetch them in, yea more, entreateth, beseecheth, commandeth, threateneth.

But you will say, Is it possible, that I should be forgiven, that have committed so many sins, so great, so heinous, and continued so long in them? I answer, Yes, it is possible. Mark that text, 1 Cor. vi. 9: the apostle reckons up as great sins as can be named, and then adds, "And such were some of you, but ye are washed." You see what kind of people were forgiven; whence we may gather, that those who are guilty of such sins may be forgiven now as well as then: "such were some of you." Whosoever thou art, it is no matter what thou hast been; all the matter is what thou wilt be. If any of the old prophets should come to thee, or any man in particular, and say, Wilt thou be content now to turn to God? if thou wilt, all thy sins shall be washed away, and thou shalt be made a heir of heaven,—it would cause him that hath any ingenuousness, to relent and say, Lord, canst thou now be so merciful to me as to forgive me after all this? Lo, Lord, I will return unto thee!

I ask thee this question, Art thou content to quit all thy sins immediately, upon assurance of being received if thou dost? If thou answerest, No, art thou not worthy to be destroyed? if, Yes, is not this assurance great comfort?

But some one may say, If heaven's gate stand thus wide open, I may come and be welcome at any time. Thou vile wretch, that darest to have such a thought! Dost thou not know that every such refusal of such an offer is so dangerous, that it may put thee into hazard of never having the like again? If the gate of heaven stood thus always open, why then did God swear in his wrath concerning some Israelites, "that they should never enter into his rest?" And what was the reason that it was said of those who were invited to the feast, but refused to come, that they should never taste of it? The master of the feast was full of wrath at the refusal of his offer, both because his kindness was despised, and also because his favour was of such great value; and shall not God be offended with those who refuse the kingdom of heaven, and the precious blood of Christ? Therefore, whensoever such an offer is made and refused, God is exceedingly angry. There goes an axe and a sword with this offer, to cut down every tree that will not bring forth good fruit. Say not when you hear of this offer, I am glad there is such a thing, I will accept of it another time, but it comes too soon for me now. Consider this, that the end of the coming of the Lord Jesus, was not only to save the souls of men; if only so, then indeed this might have been done at any time, even at the last: but his end also was, "That he might purify unto himself a peculiar people, zealous of good works," Tit. ii. 14; to purchase to himself a people that should serve him in their life time; which is a greater end than that mentioned before in the verse, "to redeem us from all iniquity." And canst thou think, that thou who hast served thy lusts all thy life time, shalt yet be accepted at death? Perhaps it is a common saying with you, If a man be called at the eleventh hour, he shall be received. It is true, if thou art called then for the first time, as the thief, who was not called before, and was then accepted; but what if thou hast been called before, and hast not accepted, but put off till death? thy case then will be exceedingly dangerous. Again, I ask thee, what is it that makes thee resolve to repent at death? If love to Christ, then it would cause thee to repent sooner; if love to thyself, how shall such a conversion be accepted?

Sec. VI. SIN THE CAUSE OF ALL CALAMITIES.

2 CHRON. VII. 14.

F MY PEOPLE, WHICH ARE CALLED BY MY NAME, SHALL HUMBLE THEMSELVES, AND PRAY, AND SEEK MY FACE, AND TURN FROM THEIR WICKED WAYS; THEN WILL I HEAR FROM HEAVEN, AND WILL FORGIVE THEIR SIN, AND WILL HEAL THEIR LAND.

WE have in these words three points:

I. That all calamities and troubles proceed from sin. This I observe from the order of the words: God first forgives their sins, then heals their land.

II. That if calamities be removed, and sins be not forgiven, they are removed in judgment, not in mercy.

III. That if sin be once forgiven, the calamity will soon be taken away.

I. All calamity is from sin, every trouble from transgression. In the chain of evils, sin is the first link that draws on all the rest, as grace is in the chain of blessings and comforts. Consider this in all kinds of judgments, which we reduce to three heads.

1. Temporal calamities are all from sin, both public and private. What was the cause of Solomon's troubles? The Lord stirred up an adversary against him, because he departed from the Lord, and had set up idolatry. So the sword departed not from David's house, because of his sin with Bathsheba, and the murder of Uriah. So the prophet tells Asa, " Because thou hast not relied on the Lord, henceforth thou shalt have war," 2 Chron. xvi. 8, 9. I could give many similar instances.

2. Spiritual judgments are from sin: these are much more grievous than the former; when a man is given up to his lusts, and to hardness of heart. These proceed from some other sins that went before; and it is a sure rule, that you never see a man given up to work uncleanness with greediness, or any open scandalous sins, but the first rise of it was his unconscionable walking with God in secret; as the apostle Paul says of the gentiles, that because, " when they knew God, they glorified him not as God," he gave them up to vile affections, Rom. i. 20—24. So Psa. lxxxi. 11, 12, " But my people would not hearken to my voice, and Israel would none of me. So I gave them up unto their own hearts' lusts, and they walked in their own counsels. As if he had said, I used all the means, but they still refused, and would none of me, and therefore I gave them up. Seest thou a man given up to a lust, his heart so cemented to it that he cannot live without it, know this is in judgment to him for some unconscionable walking before, and not practising according to his knowledge.

3. There is yet a judgment beyond these, when the Lord withdraws himself from a man; which, though men do little account of, is the most fearful of all judgments. The loss of God's presence is an incalculable loss. A man that makes wealth or honour his god, if you take that prop from him, how doth his heart sink within him! how much more, when the true God departs from a man! That God, who is the God of all comfort, if he be withdrawn, the heart sinks into a bottomless pit of horror; as, when the sun is gone, all things are covered with darkness. All true comfort springs from some measure or degree of God's presence, though men do not take notice of it; and when it is taken away, there

THE GOLDEN SCEPTRE. 239

remains nothing but horror and despair. When God had departed from Saul, 1 Sam. xvi. 14, he from that day ran into one error after another in his government, till he was destroyed: and the cause of this was sin; he had cast off the Lord, and therefore the Lord rejected him. The like was Cain's case; his judgment was, to be banished from the presence of the Lord, which he acknowledged to be a punishment, which he was not able to bear, Gen. iv. 13.

Use 1. When any trouble is upon thee, look to the inward root of it; look to sin as the cause, and thou shalt find it so. It may be the immediate cause and instrument is some outward thing, some enemy, some sickness, &c. But who hath permitted them to work? is it not the Lord? and what is the motive of his permission but sin? Men may have many several motives to do this or that, but nothing moves the Lord but sin and grace. When an enemy comes upon thee, say not, This man is the cause of this evil; but, The Lord hath suffered him to work, and sin hath occasioned this suffering. Shishak was but the vial through whose hands God poured out his wrath; 2 Chron. xii. 5, 7; so I may say, sickness is but the vial, it is the Lord's wrath that is poured out in it. Amend this common error; for men are ready to seek out the natural causes of the evils that befall them: if it be sickness, they look to such a circumstance in diet, or cold, as the cause of it; so if they miscarry in any enterprise, what folly and oversight hath been the cause of it. These are but the natural and immediate causes; but christians should look to and seek out for the supernatural. When there came a famine upon the land of Judah for three years, 2 Sam. xxi. 1, the natural cause was evident, which was a great drought, for that famine was healed by rain afterwards, and in those hot countries famine came by drought alone; but David rested not here, but went to the Lord, and inquired the reason, the sin that was the cause of it, and God told him it was for "the sin of Saul and his bloody house, because he slew the Gibeonites." Wise statesmen, when they find a mean person in a treason, rest not there, but search out who was the contriver of the plot. When Jacob saw the angels descend and ascend, he looked to the top of the ladder, and saw the Lord there, sending them to and fro. Look not to the steps of the ladder, one or two that are next to thee, but to the top of the ladder, and there thou shalt see the Lord sending one angel to afflict thee, another to preserve thee. If you say, How shall I know for what sin it is? Pray earnestly, and inquire as David did, and as Joshua did, when they saw the people flee before their enemies, that God would reveal to thee the particular sin: and if thou canst not find out the particular sin, for it may be some sin long ago committed, or some secret sin, yet be sure that sin is the cause of it; for as in the works of nature, we know the vapours arise out of the earth, and ascend invisibly, but come down again in storms and showers which we are able to see, and are sensible of, so the judgments may be open and manifest enough, but not the sins, but some secret sin that past by thee without notice may be the cause of it.

Use 2. Learn hence to see sin in its own colours. Sin is a secret and invisible evil, and in itself, as abstractedly considered, is difficult to be seen even by the most experienced, therefore, look upon it as it is clothed with calamities; and when you view it under the clothing, you will have another opinion of it than you had before. If you should know a man, who, wheresoever he comes, doth nothing but mischief, poisons one, stabs another, and leaves everywhere some marks of his villany, how hateful and terrible would he be to you! It is sin that commits all these evils among us. If sin come upon a man clothed and armed with God's wrath, as it often doth at death, then it is terrible. Why do we not look upon it thus at other times? because we do not behold it in the fearful effects of it, in the wrath due to it, as we do then. Sin is always the same, but our thoughts of it are not always the same; as the body is always the same, though the shadow be greater or less. That which men now count small sins, as swearing and petty oaths, will one day be terrible. Such a sin as was committed by Ananias and Sapphira, it may be, would seem small, to you in itself alone, but see it clothed with that judgment which befel them, dying at the apostles' feet. So, see the sin of Ahab's oppressing Naboth, which some may look at but as doing a little wrong to a poor man by a great man; but see it clothed with Ahab's death, and the dogs licking his blood, and it will appear to be most heinous. See the profaneness of Nadab and Abihu, offering strange fire, in their punishment.

Use 3. Learn, that if you would have the cross removed you must remove the sin first. You may observe it in diseases, that twenty medicines may be used, and yet if you hit not right upon the cause of the disease, the patient is none the better; but if the cause be removed, the symptoms presently vanish: so when some cross is upon us, we set our heads, and hands, and friends at work to remove it, but all in vain, whilst we hit not the cause, which is sin, and whilst that continues, the cross will continue.

The reason why our peace and prosperity are

interrupted with so many crosses and troubles is, because our lives are interwoven with so many sins. The cause of God's unevenness in his dispensations of his mercy towards thee, is the unevenness of thy carriage towards him. Hast thou a healthful body, a good estate, many friends? Think not that these shall secure thee. See Adam in paradise, Solomon in his glory, David on his mountain, which he thought he made strong,—and you shall see Adam, when sin had made a breach upon him quickly made miserable; and sin bringing in upon Solomon an army of troubles; and upon David, sin bringing in upon him the hazard of his kingdom, and the rebellion of his son. Sin in a man's best estate makes him miserable; and grace in the worst estate makes a man happy. Paul with a good conscience was happy in prison; David through faith was happy at Ziklag.

But you will say, How is it, that calamities thus follow upon sin? we feel no such thing.—And thus because the punishment of sin is deferred, the hearts of men are set to do evil. I answer,

All this is to be understood with this caution, that sin when it is perfected brings forth death, and not till then. God stayed till Ahab had oppressed Naboth, and gotten possession, and then God sends the message of death to him, "What, hast thou killed, and also taken possession?" Thus Judas was a thief whilst he kept the bag, and went on in many sins in Christ's family, and Christ lets him alone; and he goes on till he had betrayed his Master; and then, when his sin was perfected, and come to its full ripeness, then at last Christ came with judgment upon him. There is a certain period of judgment, and if the Lord stay execution till then, thou hast little cause to comfort thyself; "Because sentence against

THE GOLDEN SCEPTRE. 243

an evil work is not executed speedily, therefore the heart of the sons of men is fully set in them to do evil," Eccl. viii. 11. As if the wise man should have said, You that have peace, and comfort yourselves in this, that whatsoever the word and ministers threaten, you feel nothing, yet remember that as soon as the sin is committed, the sentence goes forth: and therefore he useth the word " sentence" to express this; though it be not so speedily executed, yet it goes forth at the same time with the commission of the sin. The sentence, you know is one thing, the execution another; and many times there is, and so may be here, a long distance between the sentence of the Judge, and the execution of it; so that his meaning is, that execution is deferred. Therefore flatter not yourselves; sentence is gone forth, and execution will follow. For the amplification of this, the vision of Zechariah seems to make it good. When swearing and theft had been committed, he saw a flying roll, Zech. v. 2, 3; which is interpreted to be the curse that goeth over all the earth for him that stealeth and sweareth, ver. 3; which curse may be upon the wing long ere it seizeth on the prey, but it goes forth as soon as those sins are committed; that is, the execution may be deferred. This is further shown in the vision of the ephah, which here represents the measure of the people's iniquities; for so the angel says, " This is wickedness;" which, until it be filled, hath not the weight of lead laid upon the mouth of it, ver. 8; it being a long while ere God comes to execution, and not till their sins are full is the talent of lead laid. It signifies that then their sins are sealed up, with the weight of lead rolled upon them, that none might be lost or forgotten, but God remembers them all. And then he saw two women come, and "the wind was in their wings," ver. 9; that is, when their sins are thus full, and their measure sealed up, their judgment comes swiftly like the wind; they carry the ephah into Shinar, and there this wickedness is set upon its own base, that is, in its proper place, a place of misery, as hell is said to be Judas's own place. Sin may sleep a long time, like a sleeping debt, which is not demanded for many years, but if a man hath not an acquittance, the creditor may call for it in the end, and lay the debtor in prison. It was forty years after Saul's slaying of the Gibeonites before execution went forth, and vengeance was called for it. So Joab's sin, which he committed in slaying Abner, which was slaying innocent blood, slept all David's time, till Solomon came to the crown.

Do not therefore as improvident debtors, who suffer the suit to run on from term to term, till they have to pay both debts and charges and all, or are outlawed. Thy sins are bringing swift damnation, and it slumbers not; it is on foot already, and will overtake thee, and meet at thy journey's end, the end of thy days. Let it therefore be thy wisdom to take up the suit, and obtain a release from God betimes, else thou shalt not only pay the debt and smart for the sin itself, but for all the time of God's patience towards thee, the riches of God's patience spent, and bear all the arrears. Christ says, "I gave her space to repent, but she repented not," Rev. ii. 21. He threatened to punish her for all the time he gave her to repent in.

The next point from these words is:

II. If the calamity be removed, and the sin be not healed, it is not removed in mercy, but in judgment.

God promises first to forgive the sin, and then to

heal the land; so that if he should have healed the land without forgiveness, it had been no mercy. 1. Because sin is worse than any cross whatsoever. If the cross be removed, and the sin remain, it is a dreadful sign. When a physician gives no more medicine, and the disease is uncured, it is a sign that the case is desperate. 2. Because the Lord doth nothing in vain; if therefore an affliction doth a man no good, it must needs do him hurt; for that which doth neither good nor hurt, must needs be in vain. If the cross doth a man no good, by healing his sin, it must needs do him hurt. You will ask, What hurt? It builds him up to destruction. If you saw a corrosive applied to eat out the live flesh, and not the dead, you would say it was applied for hurt,—so, if you see an affliction that works upon the live flesh, that wounds the heart with sorrow, but takes not away the sin, such a cross you would reckon not the medicine of a friend, but the wound of an enemy.

Use. By this thou mayest judge of thine estate, and of God's love to thee, by the issue of thine afflictions. It is true, that all kinds of crosses fall alike to all; sickness and poverty come upon the godly and the wicked; the difference is only in the issue. The same sun shines upon all, but it hardens one and it softens the other, and the same wind blows upon all, but it carrieth one ship into a haven, and dasheth another against a rock. Consider, therefore, whether thy afflictions bring thee home to the Lord, or whether they drive thee from the Lord upon the rocks. It is a common observation, that when physic works not, you say the party is mortally sick; so when afflictions work not, it is a sign he is a man of death. If he that takes not an admonition from his brother, is desperately wicked, either like a swine to trample on it, or as a dog to devour," Matt. vii. 6, how much more when a man is admonished by God himself, and is worse after it! Now, every affliction is an admonition from the Lord. In Isa. v. 1—7, when God had pruned his vineyard, and it did no good, it was then at the next door to destruction, and lying waste. If therefore thou hast had some great affliction, and now it is over, think with thyself what profit and good came to thee by it. Did it come from God's providence or not? If it did, there was something he intended, and which it did intimate to thee. If thou then didst suffer it to pass by, without taking any notice of God in it, or if thou didst notice his hand in it yet art not reclaimed, God must needs be exceedingly provoked; he will suffer the tree to stand one year or so, to see if it will bring forth fruit, but if it doth not, then he will say, " Cut it down."

There are certain times wherein the Lord, by affliction, shows himself, as it were, to a man; so that a man may grope after him and feel him, and take notice what he would have. If such times pass away, and no good is done, it is no presage of health; it is but as a drop of wrath before the great storm, a crack before the ruin of the whole building. Seek not therefore in distress, so much to have the cross removed, as the sin. "Rejoice," says the apostle, "when you fall into divers temptations," James i. 2; which he would not have said, if healing the sin had not been a greater mercy than the enduring of the affliction is grievous and dolorous. If thou hast an affliction on thee, say, It is best, I will be content to endure it still, for God means me good by it. On the contrary, if thou art not afflicted, and God suffers thee to thrive in sin, it is a sign God will destroy thee; that he leaves thee waste as a vineyard, to be overgrown with briers and thorns.

III. Take away the sin, and the cross will surely follow and be taken away also; either it or the sting of it, so that it shall be as good as no cross. An affliction consists not in the bulk of it, but in the burden What is a serpent without a sting? what is a great bulk if it have little weight? God can so fashion the heart, as that it shall not feel the burden of affliction.

1. Because crosses come for sin. Indeed, some are not for sin, but for trial, for the confirmation of the gospel. Some for the glory of God, as the blindness in the blind man; some for trial only, as Abraham's offering up his son; yet for the most part they come from sin.

2. God never afflicts but for our profit. So says the apostle; our fathers after the flesh corrected us, not always for our profit, but out of passion oftentimes; but He for our profit, Heb. xii. 9. Now when God hath thereby made us partakers of his holiness, and so we have ceased from sin, then he will cease to afflict.

It was otherwise, you will say, with David; his sin was forgiven, as Nathan told him, and yet the cross was not removed, for his child died, and the sword departed not from his house. I answer, There is an exception in these two cases. 1. Of scandal, when the name of God is blasphemed; then though he may forgive the sin, yet he may go on to punish for his name's sake. 2. When we are not thoroughly humbled; for there may be true repentance when our sinful desires are not enough mortified; God doth it that the heart may be the more cleansed. Thus David cries out of his broken bones, Psa. li. 8; and why? his heart, he says, was not cleansed, and therefore he prays for "a clean heart and a right spirit."

Use. This affords matter of comfort. When any judgment is upon us, we are apt to think we shall never be rid of it: but if thou canst but get thy heart humbled, and thy sins mortified, God will take away the cross. It is wrong to say, when we are afflicted, that we shall never see better days. Why so? is not God able to remove the cross? and if the sin be removed, he will be willing also. No man is in a hard case, but he that hath a hard heart. We are apt to think in all conditions, that what is at present will always continue: if we are in prosperity, we are apt to think, as they of whom the prophet speaks, that "tomorrow will be as to-day, and much more abundant;" so if in affliction, to say also that as it is to-day it will be to-morrow, and so for ever. But know, that if you humble yourselves, and turn from your evil ways, God will take away the calamity. There is an excellent text for this, " Humble yourselves under the mighty hand of God, that he may exalt you in due time," 1 Pet. v. 6. When a man is humbled by God, let him humble himself, and then God will exalt him,—that is the due time, and he will not stay one jot longer. And that which I say of present afflictions, I say also of crosses for the future, which you may fear that your sins will bring,—THAT IF YOU HUMBLE YOURSELVES, AND TURN FROM YOUR EVIL WAYS, GOD WILL BE MERCIFUL TO YOU AND HEAL YOU.

THE END.

SOME OTHER RELATED TITLES FROM SOLID GROUND

In addition to *The Golden Sceptre* by John Preston we have several other titles to challenge you to grow in your walk with the Lord.

THE ASSURANCE OF FAITH by Louis Berkhof
BE CAREFUL HOW YOU LISTEN by Jay Adams
CHURCH MEMBER'S GUIDE by John Angell James
DIVINE PURPOSE *in Providence and Grace* by John Matthews
EXCELLENT WOMAN *as Displayed in Proverbs 31* by Anne Pratt
FAMILY AT HOME by Gorham Abbott
GLORIOUS HISTORY OF REDEMPTION by J.O. Boyd & J. G. Machen
HOME BEAUTIFUL by J.R. Miller
IMAGO CHRISTI: *The Example of Christ* by James Stalker
JESUS TEMPTED IN THE WILDERNESS by Adolphe Monod
KING'S HIGHWAY: *Lessons from the 10 Commandments* by Richard Newton
LEAVING DARKLAND: *for those who Struggle with Life* by Ed Wallen
MISSION OF SORROW: *God's Purpose in our Afflictions* by Gardiner Spring
NOTES ON GALATIANS by J. Gresham Machen
OUR SOVEREIGN GOD by Boice, Nicole, Packer, Sproul & Stott
PRAYER OF A BROKEN HEART: *on Psalm 51* by Robert Candlish
PRECIOUS SEED: *Sermons of Scots Worthies* by Brown, Chalmers, Cunningham
RISEN CHRIST CONQUERS MARS' HILL: *A Dozen Studies on Acts 17*
SERMONS FOR CHRISTIAN FAMILIES by Edward Payson
STEPPING HEAVENWARD by Elizabeth Payson Prentiss
STILL HOUR: *Communion with God in Prayer* by Austin Phelps
THOUGHTS FOR YOUNG MEN by J.C. Ryle
THOUGHTS ON PREACHING by J.W. Alexander
TRAVELS OF TRUE GODLINESS by Benjamin Keach
TRUTH MADE SIMPLE: *Attributes of God for Children* by John Todd
UNDIVIDED LOVE: *Loving and Living for Christ* by Adolphe Monod
VIRGIN BIRTH OF OUR LORD by J. Gresham Machen
WOMAN: *Her Mission and His Life* by Adolphe Monod
WORK OF THE MINISTRY by William G. Blaikie
YEARNING TO BREATHE FREE? *Immigration, Islam & Freedom* by David Dykstra
YOUNG LADY'S GUIDE by Harvey Newcomb
YOUNG PEOPLE'S PROBLEMS by J.R. Miller

www.solid-ground-books.com
205-443-0311

www.ingramcontent.com/pod-product-compliance
Lightning Source LLC
Chambersburg PA
CBHW071706160426
43195CB00012B/1595